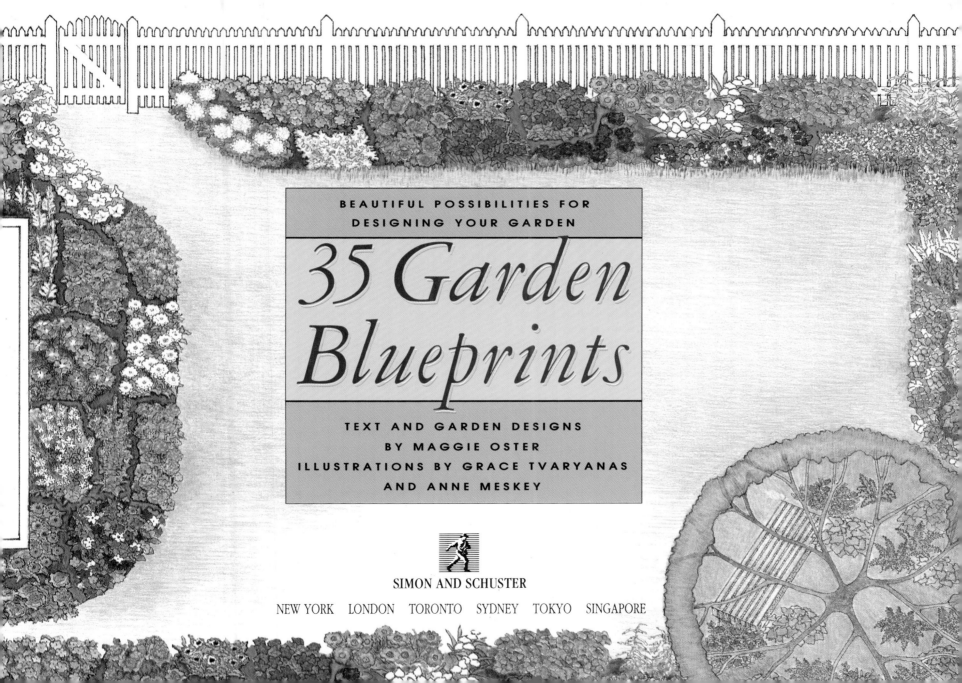

BEAUTIFUL POSSIBILITIES FOR
DESIGNING YOUR GARDEN

35 Garden Blueprints

TEXT AND GARDEN DESIGNS
BY MAGGIE OSTER
ILLUSTRATIONS BY GRACE TVARYANAS
AND ANNE MESKEY

SIMON AND SCHUSTER

NEW YORK   LONDON   TORONTO   SYDNEY   TOKYO   SINGAPORE

A FRIEDMAN GROUP BOOK

Copyright© 1989 by Michael Friedman Publishing Group, Inc.

Published by Simon and Schuster
A Division of Simon & Schuster Inc.
Simon & Schuster Building
Rockefeller Center
1230 Avenue of the Americas
New York, New York 10020

SIMON AND SCHUSTER and colophon are registered trademarks of Simon & Schuster Inc.

35 GARDEN BLUEPRINTS: Beautiful Possibilities for Designing Your Garden
was prepared and produced by
Michael Friedman Publishing Group, Inc.
15 West 26th Street
New York, New York 10010

Art Director: Mary Moriarty
Production Manager: Karen L. Greenberg

3   5   7   9   10   8   6   4   2

Library of Congress Cataloging in Publication Data

Oster, Maggie
    35 garden blueprints : beautiful possibilities for designing your
garden / text and garden designs by Maggie Oster ; illustrations by
Grace Tvarynas and Anne Meskey.
        p.   cm.
    ''A Friedman Group book''—T.p. verso.
    Bibliography: p.
    Includes index.
    ISBN 0-671-66671-1
    1. Landscape gardening—United States. 2. Gardens—United States-
-Design and plans. I. Title. II. Title: Thirty-five garden
blueprints.
SB473.O86 1989   88-23581
712'.6—dc19   CIP

Typeset by I, CLAVDIA
Color separations by South Sea International Press Ltd.
Printed and bound in Hong Kong by Leefung-Asco Printers Ltd.

Excerpt page 34–35 from H. Lincoln Foster and Laura Louise Foster's ROCK GARDENING: A Guide to Growing Alpines and Other Wildflowers in the American Garden, published by Timber Press in 1982.

For the dream, the reality,
and especially the friends
of LaNapoule.

Acknowledgments

This book would never have seen the light of day without the special
vision and guidance of Karla Olson. Her spirit, enthusiasm,
understanding, and ability to encourage make her an editor for whom I
would always be willing to go that extra mile.

The beauty of this book was dependent on the ability of Grace
Tvaryanas and Ann Meskey to interpret my plans into the drawings that
evoke the quality of the gardens that I had envisioned. They achieved
this beyond all my expectations, and I am deeply indebted.

There are always friends and family who lend support during the
birthing of a book. They know who they are and that they are loved.
There was also Joe Cocker, Robert Cray, and the antique Marantz and
Phillips. Rock and roll never lets you down.

Introduction
Page 6

The Garden Blueprints

Introduction

Gardening satisfies many needs in us, and we garden for many reasons. Perhaps we want to increase the value of our property or have pest-free food to eat, flowers for endless exuberant bouquets, or herbs for cooking and crafts. Maybe we want an excuse to get outdoors and do physical work or have time to ourselves. The vision of creating a sylvan retreat filled with flowers where we can escape the pressures of daily life motivates many of us, too.

Whatever our original motivation, I think that eventually most of us come around to gardening simply in response to the joy brought by its beauty and hope and the fascination from its possibilities. No person is more filled with faith and courage than one who gardens, and gardeners are surrounded by daily miracles. The thought that a tiny seed can become a tree or flower or food seems sheer madness, yet it happens with amazing regularity.

Gardening has helped me learn to persevere through adversity, disappointments, and frustrations—both with gardening itself and other aspects of my life. Whether living in an apartment in Manhattan, a house in the suburbs of Seattle, or on a farm in Indiana, I have always gardened. Because gardening is the basis for much of my profession, there are times when it ceased to be "fun." Fortunately now, I have reached a point where work and play have melded into one. Even if I were to go into a totally unrelated type of work, I know there would still be a garden in my life.

I don't expect everyone to approach gardening with unlimited time or zeal. There are too many fascinating avenues to explore in this life—and bills to pay. Yet I really would like to encourage people to have more than a few perfunctory trees and shrubs in the yard. There are amazing rewards, both tangible and intangible, that you would never expect from developing a garden.

Over the years I've found that the greatest enjoyment is derived when the garden itself is well planned and designed. Compare it to cooking: You probably wouldn't start a meal without at least one recipe or some idea of what you want the final result to be. Sure, sometimes you're successful anyway, but usually it's an accident. The best efforts consistently start with a plan.

When considering your yard and how to plan and plant it, remember that first and foremost, beauty is in the eye of the beholder. No two people will ever design a garden the same way. You have to take into consideration your own specific needs and preferences. Look at various gardens and pictures of gardens to get a feel for what you like and dislike. Consider how you want to use your yard. How much time and money do you want to invest in it? Will you be entertaining there often? Will weeding and watering be a means of relaxation or a chore? Do you need areas for children or pets to play in? Are there unsightly views that will have to be screened? Is there a special aspect you've always wanted, such as alpine plants, wildflowers, or a greenhouse?

You'll also have to take into consideration your growing conditions. What type of soil do you have? Is it wet or dry, clay or sand? Is the drainage bad? What's the pH of the soil? What climate zone do you live in? How much rainfall does your area receive? What are the sunlight and wind conditions in your yard? If these types of questions immediately throw you into a tizzy, don't panic. There's help available.

The greatest resource is the Cooperative Extension Service. This is a government agency available to everyone in every county of the United States. Each office has either an agricultural or a horticultural specialist who is there to provide information and assistance. These offices have a number of free or inexpensive publications on gardening. Many offices also have a Master Gardener program, which is a volunteer system of experienced gardeners. Usually the Cooperative Extension Service offices are listed under ''county'' or ''county government'' in the phone book. Your tax dollars pay for this, use it!

Other sources of information include nurseries and garden centers, other gardeners, horticultural societies, and books and magazines. Obviously, you have inherent good judgment, taste, and common sense—you bought this book!

Unfortunately, using this book alone will not ensure that your garden will be splendid. What I hope it gives you is a reliable frame of reference for some basic types and styles of gardening. There is no one quintessential Italian, Victorian, or any other garden. I have tried to include the basic elements indicative of a certain type or style. By studying these elements and the ways I've interpreted them as well as looking at other books and gardens and analyzing your wants and needs, you will be ready to either develop your own plan or work with a landscape-design professional.

Developing a plan

Once you have begun to get a general feel for what you want in a garden, you need to consider the amount of money you have to spend and the time frame in which you want to accomplish your goals. With an overall plan at your disposal, you will see logical sections to work on as funds and time permit. Each portion will be part of a cohesive whole. The end result will be unified rather than a mishmash. This doesn't mean changes can't be made; a good plan will allow for flexibility and development.

At this stage, you can either proceed to develop the plan yourself or hire a landscape designer or architect. In choosing a design professional, shop around. Talk with different designers and their clients. You want your money to be well spent and the resulting environment to be to your satisfaction. Choose someone with whom you feel comfortable and in whom you have confidence.

If you are developing your own plan, you'll first need a scale drawing of your site. Perhaps a survey map or deed description already exists. If not, use a tape measure to measure the property and all existing structures, fences, and so forth as well as natural features. Then transfer these dimensions to paper.

The basic equipment needed for this process includes graph paper with a scale of .125 inch (3 millimeters) equaling 1 foot (30 centimeters); a pencil with very fine lead, an eraser, a three-sided architects' rule, a triangle, a compass, and tracing paper. I've found most of these items either at art- or engineering-supply stores. A drawing board is handy—an inexpensive solution is a large kitchen cutting board or piece of plywood covered with poster board.

The scale used for the plans in this book varies from .5 inch (12 millimeters) equaling one foot (30 centimeters) to .09 inch equals one foot (30 centimeters); each plan is marked accordingly. When adapting one of these plans to your yard, you can use the same scale or change it to the scale you've chosen for your plan. For example, .5-inch (12 millimeters) scale readily transfers to .125-inch (6 millimeters) scale by dividing each increment in half. To enlarge .25-inch (6 millimeters) scale to .5-inch (12 millimeters), double each space.

I've used varying scales because some of the gardens are larger than others. A plan that encompasses a large backyard-type plan is in a smaller scale than an intimate little area. You'll often find it makes sense to create your overall plan in one scale and then do separate sections in another one. For most yards, if the overall plan was in .5-inch (6 millimeters) scale you would need an enormous sheet of paper; using a smaller scale makes the actual drawing a manageable size. Conversely, it's easier to work on the details of portions of your garden with a "blow-up" of an area in a larger scale.

Establishing, then transferring the various levels of your site to paper is the most difficult aspect of developing your own plan. To establish the grade of a slope, use a carpenters' level placed on a straight edge. The difference in height between the end off the ground and the ground itself expressed as a percentage indicates the *fall*, or *grade*. These amounts can be expressed on a plan as contour lines; indicate the elevation in feet or metrically measured from an established base point. All in all, this is not an easy process. Fortunately, most lots are relatively flat. If you have a particularly com-

GRACE TVARKANAS

plicated lot, consider hiring someone at least to prepare the site plan.

Once you have the site plan, you are ready to begin the process of drawing your garden plan. Put a piece of tracing paper over the site plan. Make a site analysis of your yard, including good and bad views, prevailing winds, sunny and shady areas, wet and dry areas, slope, structures, and so forth.

Remove this sheet and put down another sheet of tracing paper. On this sheet, make a rough sketch of the various elements you want to include in your yard, such as fences, hedges,

pools, a rock garden, a greenhouse, a play area, a patio, a gazebo, and the like.

Use common sense and your research to help you determine where these various elements should be. Many of these features will fit naturally in certain places. Keep in mind the seven basic design principles—*simplicity, unity, harmony, balance, scale, proportion,* and *point of focus or interest*—to assist you in making decisions.

Now replace this rough sketch with another piece of tracing paper, keeping the rough one close at hand. Begin to more accurately draw to

scale the various major elements of your garden. As these become satisfactory to you, begin determining what plants you want to include.

The plants recommended in this book were chosen for their wide adaptability and reliability as well as appearance. As much as possible, I selected plants that are seldom bothered by pests and have landscape value much of the year.

Unless otherwise noted, these plans utilize plants able to withstand winter temperatures ranging from a mimimum of 10 degrees F (–12 degrees C) to at least -30 degrees F (–34 degrees C). Most will also grow well in areas with a

winter minimum of 20 degrees F (–6 degrees C). Climates warmer than this are so specialized that gardeners in those areas will need to consult other sources.

I have included some suggestions for alternatives in various regions to help you adapt these plans. Gardeners in the minimum range 10 to 20 degrees F (–12 degrees to –6 degrees C) have a wealth of plant material from which to choose; avail yourself of these riches by studying regional publications, visiting local nurseries and garden centers, and by talking with people in your area.

Making it happen

A design plan is a combination of structural elements and plants. Experiment on paper with different combinations and configurations. It's much easier and cheaper to make changes now. Set it aside and bring it out again several times until you really feel good about the plan.

When you feel satisfied, you're ready to begin the process of installing the *hard landscape,* or structural elements. Building walls, paths, decks, and so forth seems like great fun to some people and an insurmountable task to others. Your skill level, time, confidence, and funds will be factors to consider in determining what you do. There are many excellent books on these subjects and you can utilize the resources of do-it-yourself supply centers if you're interested in getting involved.

In hiring someone to do the work, check out credentials and obtain references. When appropriate, obtain bids. Cost and quality do not always go hand in hand, but it happens frequently enough to make one realize the cheapest bid is not always the best.

Finally, you're ready to begin planting. Again, this can be done by you or hired out. The plants recommended in this book are all available from major mail-order sources, so anyone anywhere can have these gardens. Well-stocked local nurseries and garden centers will have most of the plants, also. Locally bought plants are usually larger in size than mail-ordered ones.

Most of the plans in this book require that you work up a planting area first. In the best of all possible worlds, you would till an area in the fall before planting the following spring; this allows weeds and grass to decompose during the winter and soil texture to improve. If that is not feasible, then remove the grass or plants before tilling in the spring. Either way, dig or till at least to 6 inches (15 centimeters) deep and preferably to a depth of 10 to 12 inches (25 to 30 centimeters) just before planting, incorporating a substantial amount of peat moss, compost, or dehydrated composted manure.

Plants bought bare-root from a mail-order nursery are usually planted in early spring near the last frost date. Balled-and-burlapped plants or ones growing in containers can be planted almost any time during the growing season. Watering is always crucial to successful transplanting, but this is especially true for plants transplanted during the height of summer. For the first year, give the soil a thorough soaking at least once a week—more often if necessary, if the leaves show signs of wilting.

If prepared well, there will probably be enough fertility in the soil for the first year, particularly for trees and shrubs. Annuals, perennials, bulbs, and roses will grow best with monthly feedings the first year. If foliage becomes pale and unhealthy looking during the summer, use a balanced fertilizer applied at the manufacturer's recommended rate.

One of the best methods for reducing garden maintenance is mulching because it inhibits weeds and conserves soil moisture. In areas that will probably only get planted once, such as a border of trees and shrubs (as opposed to a bed of annuals or perennials), the fabric mulches are a real work-saver. Depending on the situation, these are either put down before or after planting, then covered with a decorative mulch such as stone chips or bark. Fabric mulches allow water to pass through but not weed growth. I use a thick layer of bark chips alone, but because the bark decompostion requires nitrogen I have to use extra fertilizer.

You might think that now your garden is done, but let us hope it never will be. As living entities, plants grow, die, and constantly change. A planting that seemed right at one time will cry out for an updating later. Your own tastes and needs will evolve. There are thousands of plants and garden styles to try. By having a good plan as a starting point, you will take delight and pleasure in the evolution of your garden.

For example, in my present garden the boundaries and major framework, or structure, of the garden—which includes a split-rail fence, planting beds, decks, walks, a retaining wall, and steps—was established first. Then the main trees and shrubs were placed within those areas. Finally, with these well-defined planting areas, I can indulge in my tendency to collect and experiment with plants. I love buying the weird, strange, unusual, and little known. By remaining true to the basic design principles, I can continue to add a variety of plants—such as annuals, perennials, roses, vegetables, bulbs, herbs, and small shrubs—without losing the overall form of the garden.

This would not work for everyone and does not always work perfectly for me. Some plants have had to be moved or done away with. The moral is to plan before installing garden features or purchasing plants but remain open to the possibilities of new or different plants and garden areas. They are what make gardening an exciting and challenging adventure.

A Formal Perennial Garden

In the late 1800s and early 1900s, two English garden designers established a new style of gardening that has now become synonymous with perennial gardens. William Robinson and Gertrude Jekyll transformed the blowsy English cottage garden, with its abundance of flowers, into a tightly structured framework of hedges, walls, and paths.

One of the factors making their garden designs successful was that gardeners were hired just to trim, weed, stake, and do the other necessary chores. Few of us can afford this luxury today, but a formal perennial garden is not beyond reach. By selecting hedge plants that need only minimal pruning and a few choice perennials with very reliable growth and a long period of bloom, you can create a formal garden that fits today's time constraints and budget limitations.

This garden is for an area that is either in full sun or receives at least 5 to 6 hours of sun each day. My choice for the hedge is one of the shrubby cinquefoil (*Potentilla*) varieties, such as 'Gold Drop,' 'Goldfinger,' 'Gold Star,' or 'Katherine Dykes.' These are extremely hardy, have no pests, thrive in a wide range of soils, grow only 3 feet (.91 meter) tall, and have showy yellow flowers during the summer.

Depending upon the climate, some of the other plants used for hedges include certain varieties of barberry, holly, yew, juniper, privet, Oregon holly-grape, nandina, arborvitae, and mugho pine. For help in making a selection, consult a reliable nursery in your area.

In choosing plants for a hedge, be sure to select ones that need only minimal pruning. The supersheared look is time-consuming and, in most situations, is not nearly as attractive as natural, graceful shapes.

To extend the season of this garden, interplant with daffodils and yellow crocuses and tulips. Some other yellow-flowering plants are *Aurinia saxatilis, Euphorbia epithymoides, Alchemilla vulgaris, Kniphofia tritoma, Asclepias tuberosa, Corydalis lutea,* solidago, *Thermopsis villosa,* trollius, and verbascum.

The symmetry of the arrangement of the plants and the monochromatic color sceme of yellows and golds intensifies the formal effect, with the touch of red giving it some extra dash. Jekyll once wrote, "Suddenly entering the gold garden, even on the dullest day, will be like coming into sunshine." This garden could be the centerpiece of either a front or back yard, set in a well-manicured lawn and surrounded at a distance with taller shrubs and trees.

Of the thousands of daylily varieties available, 'Stella d'Oro' has been received most favorably by gardening experts. It begins blooming when very young and blooms exuberantly over a longer period than any other daylily. The varieties of blanket flower, yarrow, coneflower, and coreopsis suggested have a reputation as exceptional low-maintenance plants. If you can't find either of the two varieties of lily recommended, select another 2-to 2.5-foot (60 to 76 centimeter) yellow variety with dark markings.

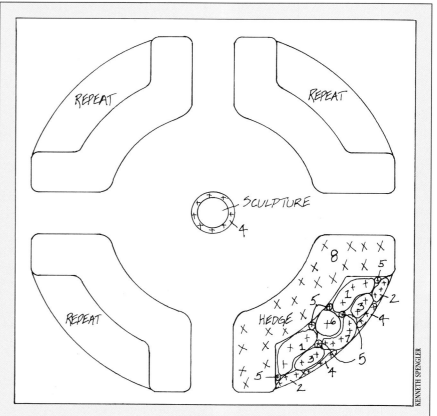

KENNETH SPENGLER

Plant List
(number of plants needed in parentheses)

1. Daylily, *Hemerocallis* 'Stella d'Oro' (24)
2. Blanket flower, *Gaillardia x grandiflora* 'Goblin' (24)
3. Yarrow, *Achillea taygetea* 'Moonshine' (8)
4. Variegated thyme, *Thymus vulgaris* 'Aureus' (32)
5. Lily, *Lilium* 'Candy Cane' or 'Freckles' (24)
6. Coneflower, *Rudbeckia fulgida* 'Goldsturm' (4)
7. Threadleaf coreopsis, *Coreopsis verticillata* 'Zagreb' (20)
8. Shrubby cinquefoil, *Potentilla fruticosa* (32)

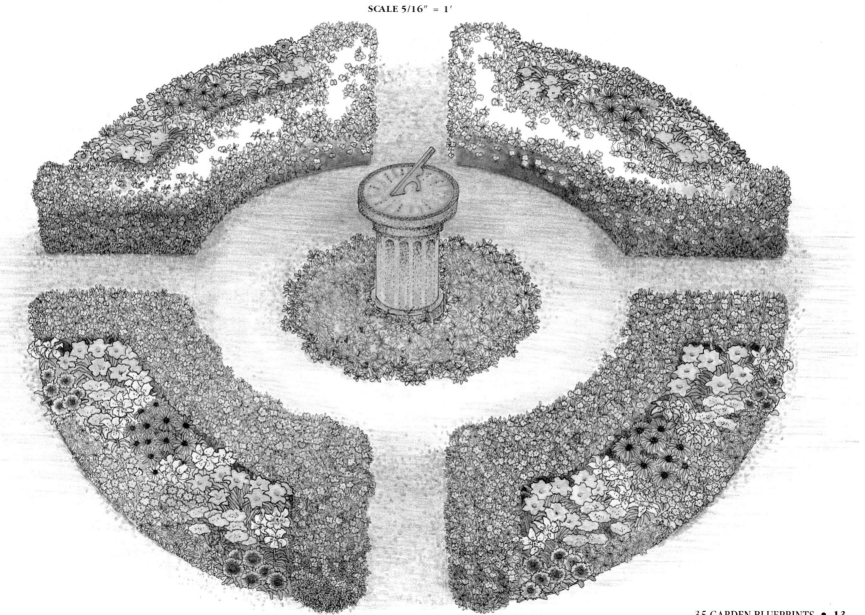

GRACE TVARYANAS

An Informal Perennial Garden

Garden design styles began taking a radical departure from tradition during the late 1930s. One style of contemporary design that has evolved from this period has been described as "asymmetrically geometric." This style features square- or rectangular-shaped beds placed in an irregular, or uneven, pattern.

Shown here as part of a paved patio area adjacent to the house, the same beds could just as readily be placed on a lawn. Another way to use the design would be to set it in a part of the yard at a distance from the house or lawn and, perhaps, add an arbor over a portion to provide light shade for a table and chairs.

An advantage to this design is that individual beds can be added as time and budget permit. You might want to prepare all the beds, plant some of them with perennials, and put annuals in the others the following year.

This plan basically incorporates plants that grow best in full sun or need at least 5 to 6 hours of sun daily. Many, however, will tolerate light shade—especially those in the upper-right-hand corner bed. If you plant under the eaves of the house, be aware that this area will probably not get much rainfall; you'll need to provide extra water here.

This is a garden with some rather dramatic touches, and it will bloom from June to October. Utilizing a wide variety of plants in a rather small area, it will appeal to the person who wants a little bit of everything. The varieties chosen are among the best available, and they're worth the search at garden centers or through mail-order companies. They were chosen because most of them have a long period of bloom, few pest problems, seldom need staking, provide flowers for cutting, and can withstand somewhat dry conditions.

By giving a little extra attention to this garden, such as working plenty of organic matter into the soil when preparing the beds and watering and fertilizing regularly during the growing season, you will make it spectacular. The most important maintenance is to remove the faded flowers, as this encourages repeat bloom on many of the plants.

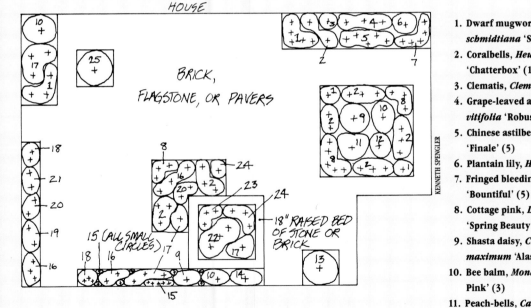

Plant List
(number of plants needed in parentheses)

1. Dwarf mugwort, *Artemesia schmidtiana* 'Silver Mound' (10)
2. Coralbells, *Heuchera sanguinea* 'Chatterbox' (18)
3. Clematis, *Clematis patens* 'Nelly Moser' (1)
4. Grape-leaved anemone, *Anemone vitifolia* 'Robustissima' (3)
5. Chinese astilbe, *Astilbe chinenesis* 'Finale' (5)
6. Plantain lily, *Hosta* 'Halcyon' (1)
7. Fringed bleeding-heart, *Dicentra* 'Bountiful' (5)
8. Cottage pink, *Dianthus plumarius* 'Spring Beauty' (11)
9. Shasta daisy, *Chrysanthemum maximum* 'Alaska' (2)
10. Bee balm, *Monarda didyma* 'Croftway Pink' (3)
11. Peach-bells, *Campanula persicifolia* 'Telham Beauty' or 'Caerulea' (1)
12. Purple coneflower, *Echinacea purpurea* 'Bright Star' (1)
13. Martha Washington's plume, *Filipendula rubra* 'Venusta' (1)
14. Globe thistle, *Echinops humilis* 'Taplow Blue' (1)
15. Oriental lily, *Lilium* 'Oriental Hybrids Mixed' (12)
16. Catmint, *Nepeta Mussinii* 'Blue Wonder' (9)
17. Balloon flower, *Platycodon grandiflorus* var. *Mariesii* (8)
18. Lamb's-ears, *Stachys byzantina* (3)
19. Showy stonecrop, *Sedum spectabile* 'Carmine' (2)
20. Speedwell, *Veronica spicata* 'Icicle' (4)
21. Yarrow, *Achillea Millefolium* 'Roseum' (2)
22. Cranesbill, *Geranium Endressii* 'Wargrave Pink' (3)
23. Soapwort, *Saponaria Ocymoides* (3)
24. Stonecrop, *Sedum spurium* 'Bronze Carpet' (4)
25. Rose fountain grass, *Pennisetum alopecuroides* (1)

A Perennial Cutting Garden

One of the great joys of gardening is having fresh flowers to cut and bring indoors for yourself and friends. And don't say that you could never learn to arrange flowers! A few well-grown flowers in a sparkling crystal vase creates drama in any room.

Actually, the hardest task with a perennial cutting garden is deciding just which plants to grow. Your selection should take into account which flowers will be beautiful in the garden, as well as which will contribute to magnificent arrangements. In choosing plants for this garden, I included tall, spiky flowers to add a linear element to arrangements and larger, flatter, rounder flowers to provide mass. Other plants were chosen for their foliage or their light, airy, "filler" flowers. Another criteria that most of these plants meet is both a long period of bloom and a long cut life.

The plants chosen for this garden are in shades of pink and blue plus white. If you prefer yellow to pink, substitute *Corydalis lutea* for the *Ajuga, Achillea* 'Moonshine' for 'Roseum,' *Rudbeckia* 'Goldsturm' for centaurea, *Thermopsis montana* for the gayfeather, a white-flowered variety of the coralbells, *Doronicum caucasicum* 'Magnificum' for the painted daisy, the miniature rose 'Gold Coin' for the speedwell, and additional *Physostegia* 'Summer Snow' for 'Vivid.'

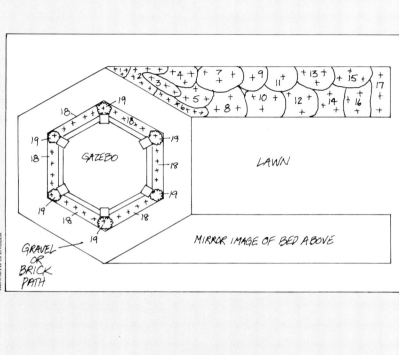

Plant List
(number of plants needed in parentheses)

1. Bugleweed, *Ajuga genevensis* 'Pink Beauty' (6)
2. Speedwell, *Veronica* 'Blue Fox' (12)
3. False dragonhead, *Physostegia virginiana* 'Vivid' (6)
4. Painted daisy, *Chrysanthemum coccineum* (6)
5. Shasta daisy, *Chrysanthemum maximum* 'Alaska' (6)
6. Lamb's-ears, *Stachys byzantina* (12)
7. Peach-bells, *Campanula persicifolia* 'Telham Beauty' or 'Caerulea' (6)
8. Yarrow, *Achillea Millefolium* 'Roseum' (6)
9. Monkshood, *Aconitum Carmichaelii* (2)
10. False dragonhead, *Physostegia virginiana* 'Summer Snow' (6)
11. Baby's breath, *Gypsophila paniculata* 'Bristol Fairy' (2)
12. Pincushion flower, *Scabiosa caucasica* (6)
13. Bee balm, *Monarda didyma* 'Alba' or other white-flowered variety (6)
14. Persian centaurea, *Centaurea hypoleuca* 'John Coutts' (6)
15. Gayfeather, *Liatris spicata* 'Kobold' (6)
16. Balloon flower, *Platycodon grandiflorus* (6)
17. Common wormwood, *Artemisia Absinthium* 'Lambrook Silver' (6)
18. Coralbells, *Heuchera sanguinea* (24)
19. Dwarf white spruce, *Picea glauca* 'Conica' (6)

Usually perennial beds such as these will have much shorter-growing plants at the front, but since longer-stemmed flowers are preferable for arranging, the short plants were bypassed except for the triangular part of each bed.

At the turn of this century, a cutting garden was planted in rows much like a vegetable garden. It was typically placed at the far corner of the property and surrounded by a fence or hedge as it was not considered to be particularly aesthetic. Today, few of us have the time or space to devote to such a specialized area. With this in mind, I designed this garden to be reminiscent of the classic English border garden, complete with gazebo, and yet provide a large amount of material for cutting. In fact, there are enough plants here that what you cut will hardly be missed.

The inspiration for this garden and the gazebo is J. Liddon Pennock's Meadowbrook Farm, a delightful nursery and garden center in suburban Philadelphia, Pennsylvania. Pennock is known for his gazebo gardens at the annual Philadelphia Flower Show. This gazebo looks ornate but is of quite simple construction, using large timbers and off-the-shelf Victorian millwork. The finials are concrete. Use pressure-treated lumber, if possible, or treat the wood yourself with a safe wood preservative, such as copper or zinc naphthanate.

A Formal Annual Garden

GRACE TVARYANAS

The Victorian era was the heyday of the formal annual garden. The grounds of ornately trimmed houses as well as public buildings and parks were planted with large curving beds filled with hundreds of annual flowers, often of only a single variety or color.

Although sometimes considered crude and garish, such gardens still have a place in the heart of anyone who has lovingly restored a beautiful turn-of-the-century home. A wonderful modern-day example of this style of garden is the Enid A. Haupt Conservatory Garden behind the Smithsonian "castle" just off the Mall in Washington, D.C.

The simple circular garden design shown here has the requisite centerpiece for such a garden—a large cast-iron urn. A typical Victorian touch is to plant the urn with a spiky plant, such as a small yucca, pandanus, or *Dracaena marginata* surrounded by English ivy or other vine, then fill it with other flowers. In the lists, the first plant of each list is suggested as the filler. Extras of the other flowers can be added as well.

If you don't have enough space for the entire design, just create the center portion. The key to success with a formal annual garden is to select plants that will bloom all summer long without requiring removal of faded flowers.

Choosing just one color scheme was entirely too frustrating for me, what with the wealth of annual varieties available, so I have created seven color schemes for a sunny location and one for a partially shaded garden.

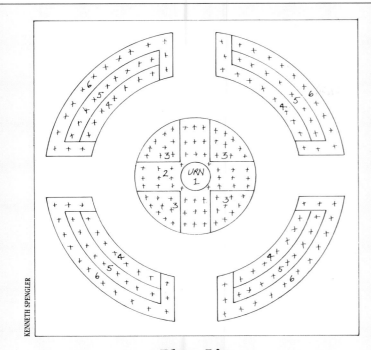

KENNETH SPENGLER

Plant List
(number of plants needed in parentheses)

WHITE GARDEN
1. Common garden petunia, *Petunia* x *hybrida* 'White Cascade' (4)
2. Flowering tobacco, *Nicotiana alata* 'Domino White'(40)
3. Geranium, *Pelargonium* x *hortorum* 'White Orbit' (36)
4. Wax begonia, *Begonia* x *semperflorens-cultorum* 'Whisky' (28)
5. Zinnia, *Zinnia elegans* 'Peter Pan White' (36)
6. Mealycup sage, *Salvia farinacea* 'Silver White' or 'White Bedder' (60)

GOLDEN GARDEN
1. Black-eyed Susan vine, *Thunbergia alata* (4)
2. Ornamental pepper, *Capsicum annuum* 'Fiesta' (40)
3. Creeping zinnia, *Sanvitalia procumbens* 'Mandarin Orange' (36)
4. Signet marigold, *Tagetes tenuifolia* 'Golden Gem' (28)
5. Garden nasturtium, *Tropaeolum majus* 'Double Dwarf Jewel Golden' (36)
6. African marigold, *Tagetes erecta* 'Perfection Gold' (60)

RED-AND-WHITE GARDEN
1. Vinca, *Catharanthus roseus* 'Polka Dot' (4)
2. Zinnia, *Zinnia elegans* 'Red Lollipop' (40)
3. Dusty-miller, *Centaurea cineraria* 'Silverdust' (36)
4. Sweet alyssum, *Lobularia maritima* 'Carpet of Snow' (28)
5. Common garden petunia, *Petunia* x *hybrida* 'Ultra Red Star' (36)
6. Cockscomb, *Celosia cristata* 'New Look' (60)

ORANGE GARDEN
1. Impatiens, *Impatiens wallerana* 'Gem Orange' (4)
2. French marigold, *Tagetes patula* 'Queen Sophia' (40)
3. Treasure flower, *Gazania rigens* 'Mini Star Tangerine' (36)
4. Garden nasturtium, *Tropaeolum majus* 'Whirlybird' (36)
5. Zinnia, *Zinnia elegans* 'Dreamland Coral' (36)
6. Cockscomb, *Celosia cristata* 'Apricot Brandy'(60)

BLUE GARDEN
1. Browallia, *Browallia speciosa* 'Jingle Bells' (4)
2. Cornflower, *Centaurea cyanus* 'Jubilee Gem' (40)
3. Phacelia, *Phacelia campanularia* (36)
4. Ageratum, *Ageratum Houstonianum* 'Blue Danube' (28)
5. Larkspur, *Delphinium* 'Dwarf Blue Butterfly' (36)
6. Mealy-cup sage, *Salvia farinacea* 'Victoria' (60)

PINK GARDEN
1. Ivy geranium, *Pelargonium peltatum* 'Summer Showers' (4)
2. Geranium, *Pelargonium* x *hortorum* 'Appleblossom Orbit' (40)
3. Common garden petunia, *Petunia* x *hybrida* 'Plum Pink' (36)
4. Wax begonia, *Begonia* x *semperflorens-cultorum* 'Gin' (28)
5. Zinnia, *Zinnia elegans* 'Rose Pinwheel' (36)
6. Flowering tobacco, *Nicotiana alata* 'Nicki Rose' (60)

SALMON-AND-PURPLE GARDEN
1. Impatiens, *Impatiens wallerana* 'Blitz Salmon' (4)
2. Scarlet sage, *Salvia splendens* 'Hotline Violet' (40)
3. Geranium, *Pelargonium* x *hortorum* 'Elite Salmon' (36)
4. Common garden petunia, *Petunia* x *hybrida* 'Ultra Salmon' (28)
5. Heliotrope, *Heliotropium arborescens* 'Marine' (36)
6. Common basil, *Ocimum basilicum* 'Purple Ruffles' (60)

SHADE GARDEN
1. Coleus, *Coleus* x *hybridus* 'Scarlet Poncho' (4)
2. Impatiens, *Impatiens wallerana* 'Scarlet Imp' (40)
3. Impatiens, *Impatiens wallerana* 'White Imp' (36)
4. Madagascar periwinkle, *Catharanthus roseus* 'Little Bright Eye' (28)
5. Wax begonia, *Begonia* x *semperflorens-cultorum* 'Pizzazz Red' (36)
6. Coleus, *Coleus* x *hybridus* 'Red Velvet' (60)

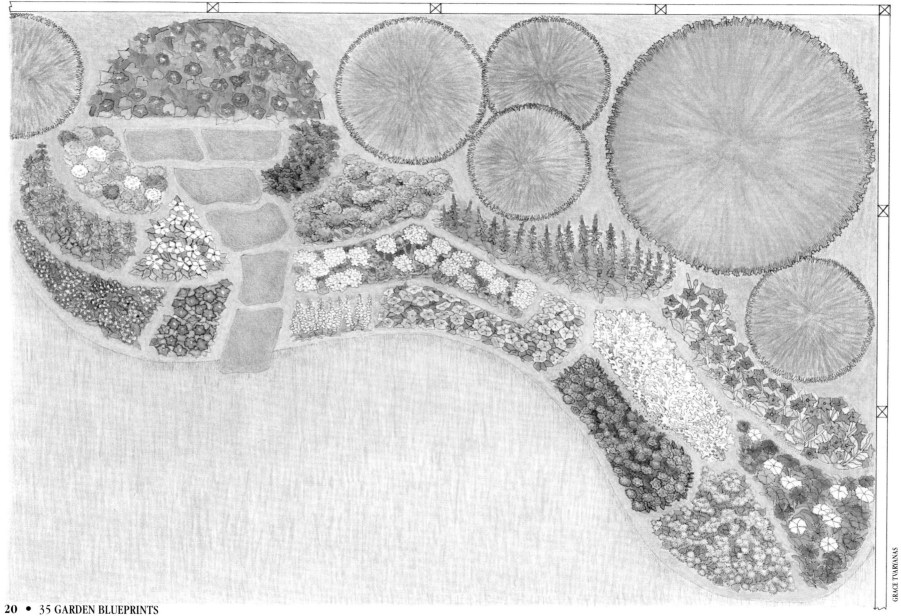

GRACE TVARYANAS

An Informal Annual Garden

No other plant group adds the exuberance of color to the garden like annual flowers. This garden plan uses those annuals that not only withstand hot temperatures and full sun but also continue blooming right up to frost.

By choosing the best of the new varieties, like the ones suggested, you'll get plants that produce flowers over a long period, have uniform growth, and are seldom bothered by pests. If you substitute, be sure to select varieties that are of similar color and grow to the same mature height.

This informal garden plan places plants in irregular drifts rather than in more rigid, geometrical forms. Flowing curves, "naturalistic" lines, and an asymmetrical approach are typical of this style of informal garden. Curves blend into one another and with the natural terrain. An informal bed such as this one could also surround a patio or be used along the edge of a front walk.

The garden shown is in front of a border planting of dwarf mugho pines and a large holly tree. A tall board fence behind these plants screens out an unsightly view. The bower covered with carmine-colored common morning-glories is an inexpensive model made

of strong steel tubing coated with weatherproof, green polyvinylchloride (PVC) so installation and maintenance is minimal. It can shelter a 4-foot (1.2-meter) garden bench or a small table and chairs.

The colors chosen for this particular design are in shades of soft reds, magentas, pinks, blues, and purples. The white flowers reflect the light and add sparkle. This combination of colors is restful and offers the world-weary person a beautiful oasis in which to relax.

An annual garden such as this one is most easily achieved by setting out plants that were either purchased at a garden center or started indoors at least six to eight weeks prior to the last frost date for your area. When planting, space the plants according to the directions on the plant label or seed packet. Stagger the plants rather than placing them directly in front of one another to achieve the casual effect you want.

A way to make this a low-maintenance garden is to mulch around the plants with a thick layer of shredded bark, compost, or other coarse, weed-free organic material. Be sure to feed and water regularly during the growing season. Use a fertilizer for flowers, such as 5–10–10.

Plant List
(number of plants needed in parentheses)

1. Common morning glory, *Ipomoea purpurea* 'Scarlet O'Hara' (12)
2. Pincushion flower, *Scabiosa atropurpurea* 'Dwarf Double Mixed' (12)
3. Scarlet sage, *Salvia splendens* 'Hotline Violet' (14)
4. Madagascar periwinkle, *Catharanthus roseus* 'Morning Mist' (16)
5. Common Garden verbena, *Verbena* x *hybrida* 'Trinidad' (11)
6. Phacelia, *Phacelia campanularia* (6)
7. Common basil, *Ocimum Basilicum* 'Purple Ruffles' (6)
8. Zinnia, *Zinnia elegans* 'Pink Splendor' (7)
9. Mealy-cup sage, *Salvia farinacea* 'Victoria' (15)
10. Flowering tobacco, *Nicotiana alata* 'Nicki Rose (16)
11. Geranium, *Pelargonium* x *hortorum* 'Orbit White' (16)
12. Common snapdragon, *Antirrbinum majus* 'Floral Carpet White' (6)
13. Common garden petunia, *Petunia* x *hybrida* 'Summer Madness' (18)
14. Dusty-miller, *Centaurea Cineraria* 'Silverdust' (12)
15. Sweet alyssum, *Lobularia maritima* 'Royal Carpet' (13)
16. Ageratum, *Ageratum Houstonianum* 'Blue Mink' (12)
17. Rainbow pink, *Dianthus cbinensis* 'Princess Mix' (14)

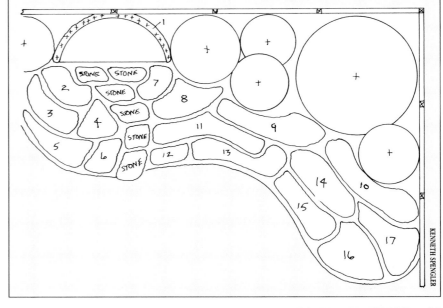

KENNETH SPENGLER

An Annual Cutting Garden

An affection for bygone days has provided the impetus for the resurgence of afternoon tea, romantic white cotton dresses, and Adirondack lawn furniture. Fitting in perfectly with this nostalgia is an annual cutting garden. All you need to complete the picture is a straw hat, flower-gathering shears, a galvanized French flowerpot for immersing fresh-cut flowers, a workbench where you can arrange the flowers, and a watering can for tending the beds. "Wellies" are optional.

Seriously, this garden plan does reflect the traditional cutting garden, with its neat rows of predominantly old-fashioned annuals. Distinguishing it from the past is the fact that it need not be relegated to a hidden spot. Rather, the varieties suggested are attractive enough to give the garden a place of prominence near the house. In this instance, the flowers are set against a 3-foot (.91-meters) tall wall just below a patio. The beds could also be placed against a fence or hedge, bordering a wall, or planted in any area receiving full sun.

The plants are arranged from shortest to tallest in each of the two beds. Most of the varieties recommended are of mixed colors and have a graceful form. With one exception, the dwarf sunflower, four or eight plants of each variety are used. Since most pre-started plants available at garden centers are in multiples of four, this simplifies shopping.

Although relatively small, this garden should provide plenty of flowers throughout the summer. You could easily expand the size, if desired.

To get the most possible flowers, prepare the beds well before planting by incorporating organic matter, such as peat moss, compost, or dehydrated composted manure. Use a fertilizer formulated for flowers, such as 5–10–10, according to the manufacturer's directions, and water the beds well at least once a week if rainfall is not adequate. Mulching around the plants with shredded bark or other material will reduce the need for watering.

The dwarf sunflowers, 3 to 4 feet (.91 to 1.2 meters), may seem an unusual choice, but they make dramatic arrangements. The African marigold variety is a nonscented one, so no one should be offended. The godetia is a new hybrid that is heat tolerant; it does not transplant well, so sow directly into the garden.

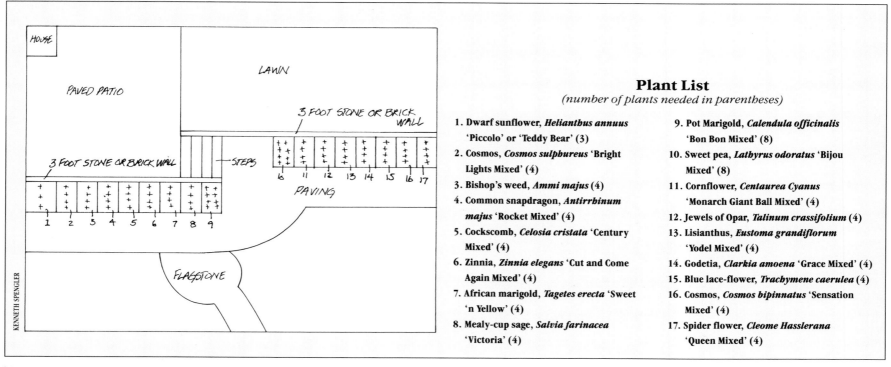

Plant List
(number of plants needed in parentheses)

1. **Dwarf sunflower, *Helianthus annuus* 'Piccolo' or 'Teddy Bear'** (3)
2. **Cosmos, *Cosmos sulphureus* 'Bright Lights Mixed'** (4)
3. **Bishop's weed, *Ammi majus*** (4)
4. **Common snapdragon, *Antirrhinum majus* 'Rocket Mixed'** (4)
5. **Cockscomb, *Celosia cristata* 'Century Mixed'** (4)
6. **Zinnia, *Zinnia elegans* 'Cut and Come Again Mixed'** (4)
7. **African marigold, *Tagetes erecta* 'Sweet 'n Yellow'** (4)
8. **Mealy-cup sage, *Salvia farinacea* 'Victoria'** (4)
9. **Pot Marigold, *Calendula officinalis* 'Bon Bon Mixed'** (8)
10. **Sweet pea, *Lathyrus odoratus* 'Bijou Mixed'** (8)
11. **Cornflower, *Centaurea Cyanus* 'Monarch Giant Ball Mixed'** (4)
12. **Jewels of Opar, *Talinum crassifolium*** (4)
13. **Lisianthus, *Eustoma grandiflorum* 'Yodel Mixed'** (4)
14. **Godetia, *Clarkia amoena* 'Grace Mixed'** (4)
15. **Blue lace-flower, *Trachymene caerulea*** (4)
16. **Cosmos, *Cosmos bipinnatus* 'Sensation Mixed'** (4)
17. **Spider flower, *Cleome Hasslerana* 'Queen Mixed'** (4)

SCALE ¹/₄″ = 1′

SCALE ¼″ = 1′

GRACE TVARYANAS

An Annual and Perennial Garden

Certain images remain forever etched in our minds—people we've known, places we've been. Old Westbury Gardens in Old Westbury, New York, is one such place for me. Among its many wonderful offerings is a lovely cottage garden composed of annuals and perennials and surrounded by a white picket fence. The garden plan illustrated here is a variation of that one, with my own favorite plants featured, including old-fashioned plants as well as some just now becoming popular.

The wide bed surrounds a portion of the house and is composed basically of sun-loving plants, although most would tolerate very light shade. This area could just as readily be placed along a straight area instead of around the corners of a building. The L-shaped bed gradually becomes a garden for partial shade. This bed is kept relatively narrow for easy access.

A picket fence allows good air circulation around the plants. You might also want to consider a rail or ornate iron fence. If you are very ambitious and the space is available, you could have a flower bed on the other side of the fence.

This garden features a profusion of color, and there will be flowers throughout the growing season. By using annuals with the perennials, you can alter the color scheme to a certain extent each year. Plants that bloom for only a short period, such as the common garden peony and Oriental poppy, are kept to a minimum and tucked in among other plants that will grow over them as the season progresses.

Installing and maintaining this garden is no small feat. You may want to do only a portion at a time or just use a segment of the design.

Plant List
(number of plants needed in parentheses)

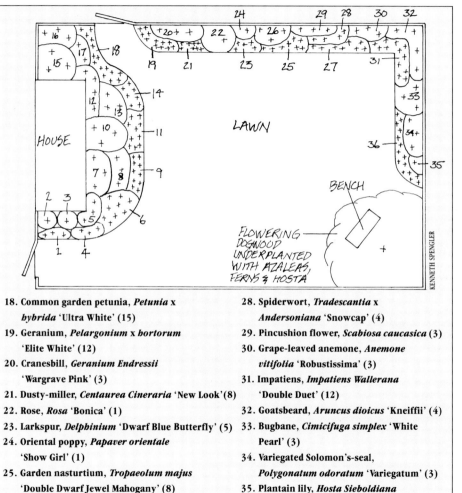

1. Japanese roof iris, *Iris tectorum* 'Alba' (3)
2. Bee balm, *Monarda didyma* 'Adam' (3)
3. Peony, *Paeonia lactiflora* 'Mme. Ducel' (3)
4. Shasta daisy, *Chrysanthemum maximum* 'Snow Lady' (1)
5. Threadleaf coreopsis, *Coreopsis verticillata* 'Sun Ray' (3)
6. Flowering tobacco, *Nicotiana alata* 'Nicki Mixed' (9)
7. Gas plant, *Dictamnus albus* (3)
8. Mealy-cup sage, *Salvia farinacea* 'Victoria' (3)
9. Geranium, *Pelargonium x hortorum* 'Elite Pink' (10)
10. Hollyhock mallow, *Malva Alcea* var. *fastigiata* (3)
11. Zinnia, *Zinnia elegans* 'Dreamland White' (10)
12. False dragonhead, *Physostegia virginiana* 'Alba' (4)
13. Showy stonecrop, *Sedum spectabile* 'Autumn Joy' (3)
14. Ageratum, *Ageratum Houstonianum* 'Royal Delft' (7)
15. Eulalia grass, *Miscanthus sinensis* 'Gracillimus' (3)
16. Yarrow, *Achillea filipendulina* 'Coronation Gold' (3)
17. Daylily, *Hemerocallis* 'Stella d'Oro' (3)

18. Common garden petunia, *Petunia x hybrida* 'Ultra White' (15)
19. Geranium, *Pelargonium x hortorum* 'Elite White' (12)
20. Cranesbill, *Geranium Endressii* 'Wargrave Pink' (3)
21. Dusty-miller, *Centaurea Cineraria* 'New Look' (8)
22. Rose, *Rosa* 'Bonica' (1)
23. Larkspur, *Delphinium* 'Dwarf Blue Butterfly' (5)
24. Oriental poppy, *Papaver orientale* 'Show Girl' (1)
25. Garden nasturtium, *Tropaeolum majus* 'Double Dwarf Jewel Mahogany' (8)
26. Balloon flower, *Platycodon grandiflorus* (3)
27. Wax begonia, *Begonia semperflorens-cultorum* 'Pizzazz Mixed' (8)

28. Spiderwort, *Tradescantia x Andersoniana* 'Snowcap' (4)
29. Pincushion flower, *Scabiosa caucasica* (3)
30. Grape-leaved anemone, *Anemone vitifolia* 'Robustissima' (3)
31. Impatiens, *Impatiens Wallerana* 'Double Duet' (12)
32. Goatsbeard, *Aruncus dioicus* 'Kneiffii' (4)
33. Bugbane, *Cimicifuga simplex* 'White Pearl' (3)
34. Variegated Solomon's-seal, *Polygonatum odoratum* 'Variegatum' (3)
35. Plantain lily, *Hosta Sieboldiana* 'Elegans' (1)
36. Impatiens, *Impatiens Wallerana* 'Shady Lady Pastel Mix Improved' (15)

A Vegetable Garden

Over the years, my vegetable gardens have ranged from a tomato in a pot to a 50-by-50-foot (15-by-15-meter) plot. Yet no matter what the size, my goal has always been to have fresh-tasting, nutritious vegetables as free of pesticides as possible. With careful planning, you can have this plus a bountiful harvest. In addition, your vegetable garden can be a handsome addition to your landscape.

As an example, the most elaborate and beautiful food garden is probably the Chateau de Villandry in France, designed as a large, formal parterre. A quick perusal of popular magazines provides lots of ideas for attractive vegetable gardens on a more realistic backyard scale.

This vegetable garden is fairly traditional in that it has the "typical" rows. Yet by adding brightly colored edible annual flowers as a border and the unusual vining malabar spinach on an arbor with a bench beneath, it provides food for the spirit as well as the body.

For a super harvest, be sure the garden gets at least 1 inch (2.5 centimeters) of water each week (consider a drip irrigation system) and feed at the recommended intervals with a vegetable garden fertilizer. Mulch to conserve water and reduce weed growth. Some of the vegetables listed will produce over a long period, while others, such as carrots and beets, have a short harvest season. Fill in the gaps from these harvests with another planting of the same crop or a different one, if you prefer. Site this garden so that the taller crops are at the northern side, with the rows running from east to west. Provide poles or bean towers for the beans and peas, cages for the tomatoes.

SCALE 5/32″ = 1′

GRACE TVARYANAS

Except for the cool-weather-loving peas and lettuce, this is basically a main-growing-season garden for a household of no more than four people. The vegetables and varieties listed for this plan are my favorites, representing both tried-and-true ones as well as the very newest. I like to have a little bit of everything, and the plant list reflects that. The annual herbs included are a flavorful complement to many of the vegetables.

Substitute with your favorite vegetables and varieties, if desired. The best planting times and varieties differ from region to region. Consult local botanical gardens or garden centers in your area for local recommendations.

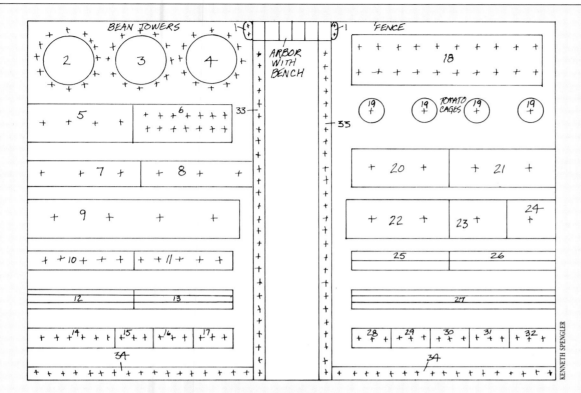

KENNETH SPENGLER

Plant List
(number of plants needed in parentheses)

1. **Malabar spinach,** *Basella alba* 'Rubra' or 'Red Stem' (4)
2. **Yard-long bean,** *Vigna unguiculata sesquipedalis* (12)
3. **Snap bean,** *Phaseolus vulgaris* 'Blue Lake' (12)
4. **Sugar snap pea,** *Pisum sativum* 'Sugar Snap' (12)
5. **Okra,** *Abelmoschus esculentus* 'Clemson Spineless' and 'Burgundy' (2 of each)

6. **Green pea,** *Pisum sativum,* 'Green Arrow' (14)
7. **Bell pepper,** *Capsicum annuum* 'Crispy,' 'Gypsy,' and 'Golden Summer' (1 of each)
8. **Hot pepper,** *Capsicum annuum* 'Mexi Bell,' 'Super Chili,' and 'Jalapeno' (1 of each)
9. **Summer squash,** *Cucurbita Pepo* var. *Melopepo* 'Sunburst,' 'Gold Rush,' 'Spineless Zucchini,' and 'Kuta' (1 of each)
10. **Broccoli,** *Brassica oleracea* 'Green Comet' (5)

11. **Purple cauliflower,** *Brassica oleracea* 'Burgundy Queen' or 'Violet Queen' (5)
12. **Carrot,** *Daucus Carota* var. *sativus* 'Lindoro' and 'A-Plus' (1 packet of each)
13. **Beet,** *Beta vulgaris* 'Pacemaker III' (1 packet)
14. **Common basil,** *Ocimum Basilicum* 'Lettuce Leaf' and 'Lemon' (3 of each)
15. **Sweet marjoram,** *Origanum Majorana* (3)
16. **Summer savory,** *Satureja hortensis* (3)

17. **Italian parsley,** *Petroselinum crispum* var. *neopolitanum* (3)
18. **Sweet corn,** *Zea Mays* 'Butterfruit' (20)
19. **Tomato,** *Lycopersicon Lycopersicum* 'San Marzano' 'Gardener's Delight,' 'Burpee's Big Girl,' and 'Yellow Pear' (1 of each)
20. **Winter squash,** *Cucurbita Pepo* var. *Pepo* 'Jersey Golden Acorn' (2)
21. **Winter squash,** *Cucurbita moschata* 'Burpee's Butterbush' (2)
22. **Cucumber,** *Cucumis sativus* 'Park's Burpless Bush' and 'Salad Bush' (1 of each)
23. **Cantaloupe,** *Cucumis Melo* 'Musketeer' (1)
24. **Watermelon,** *Citrullus lanatus* 'Burpee's Sugar Bush' (1)
25. **Kohlrabi,** *Brassica oleracea* 'Grand Duke' (1 packet)
26. **Swiss chard,** *Beta vulgaris* 'Burpee's Fordhook Giant' and 'Burpee's Fordhook Rhubarb' (1 packet each, mixed together)
27. **Garden lettuce,** *Lactuca sativa* (Mix 1 packet of each of your favorites together, such as 'Green Ice,' 'Red Sails,' 'Buttercrunch,' 'Crispy Sweet,' and 'Royal Oak Leaf.')
28. **Chive,** *Allium Schoenoprasum* (3)
29. **Garlic chive,** *Allium tuberosum* (3)
30. **Coriander,** *Coriandrum sativum* (3)
31. **Fennel,** *Foeniculum vulgare* (3)
32. **Dill,** *Anethum graveolens* 'Dukat' (3)
33. **Garden nasturtium,** *Tropaeolum majus* 'Jewel Mixed' (52)
34. **Pot marigold,** *Calendula officinalis* 'Bon Bon Mixed' (34)

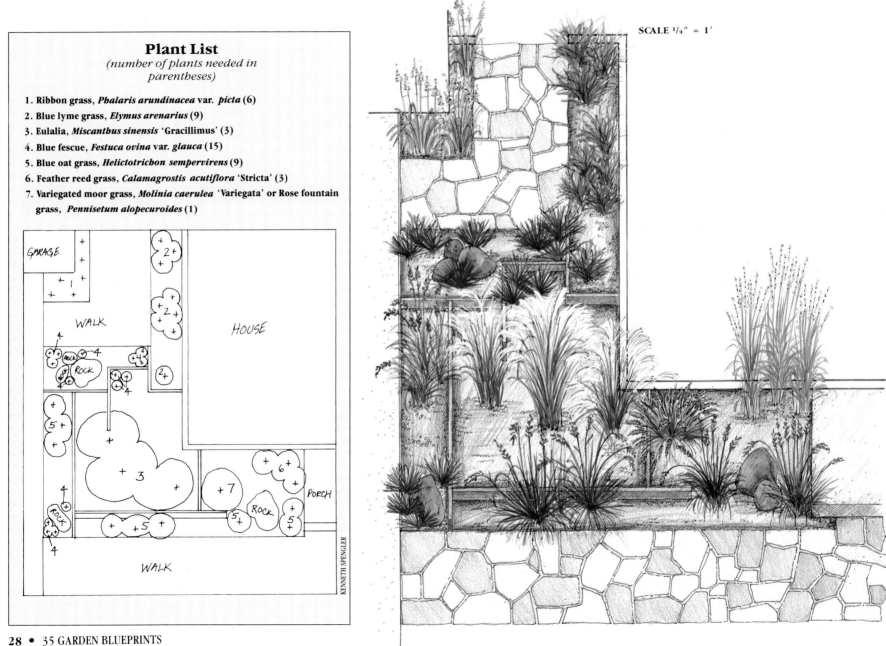

Plant List
(number of plants needed in parentheses)

1. Ribbon grass, *Phalaris arundinacea* var. *picta* (6)
2. Blue lyme grass, *Elymus arenarius* (9)
3. Eulalia, *Miscanthus sinensis* 'Gracillimus' (3)
4. Blue fescue, *Festuca ovina* var. *glauca* (15)
5. Blue oat grass, *Helictotrichon sempervirens* (9)
6. Feather reed grass, *Calamagrostis acutiflora* 'Stricta' (3)
7. Variegated moor grass, *Molinia caerulea* 'Variegata' or Rose fountain grass, *Pennisetum alopecuroides* (1)

GARAGE

WALK

HOUSE

ROCK

ROCK

ROCK

PORCH

ROCK

WALK

SCALE ¼″ = 1′

KENNETH SPENGLER

ANNE MESKEY

An Ornamental Grass Garden

Rustling and swaying in the wind, ornamental grasses enrich the landscape almost year-round as can few other plants. Add to this the fact that grasses attract almost no pests, tolerate poor, dry soils and air pollution, and need only a trim each spring, and it should come as no surprise that these are rapidly becoming the latest favorite of the gardening world.

Ornamental grasses range in height from just 6 inches (15 centimeters) to over 20 feet (6 meters). There are about twenty-five annual types, which are grown mainly for their dried flowers. The perennial grasses are preferred for landscape use. Of these, there are over two hundred varieties, with most hardy to –20 degrees F (–28 degrees C).

Some grasses have blue foliage, and many variegated forms are also available. Winter color tends toward golds and tans. Most grasses bloom in late summer or fall. Although these are wonderful to cut and dry for bouquets, be sure to leave some blooms on the plants because their effect in the winter landscape is such a plus.

How do you use ornamental grasses in the landscape? Just as you would any perennial: massed in groups of a single type; alone as an accent or specimen plant; with other perennials or with annuals and perennials in beds, borders, or islands; or in combination with evergreen and deciduous trees and shrubs.

These grasses grow in full sun to light shade. Prepare the soil by incorporating peat moss or other organic matter. Fertilize in the spring as you do your other perennials, using a formula such as 5–10–10 at the rate of about 1 to 2 pounds (.373 to .746 kilograms) per 100 square feet (9.2 square meters). Also in the spring, cut the stems of the grasses back to 6 inches (15 centimeters).

There is disagreement as to the hardiness range of grasses. Those used here are considered hardy to –30 degrees F (–34 degrees C) by some horticulturists, but there is not a consensus of opinion or any guarantees. The blue fescue does not grow well in areas with a winter minimum warmer than –10 degrees F (–23 degrees C), so in these regions substitute with liriope. If the ribbon grass turns brown by midsummer, trim it back to bring on new growth.

Both the ribbon grass and blue lyme grass spread more rapidly than the others, so they are confined in this design.

This plan is for an area between a driveway, house, and garage. By eliminating all lawn and using a fabric mulch beneath the stones, you can create a very low-maintenance garden. This plan would adapt well to an entire front foundation planting, border, or island. Use pressure-treated pine 2-by-4-inch (5-by-10 centimeter) boards with the 2-inch (5-centimeter) side up to function as the divider; stain, if desired. Use a color and type of stone that blends best with the house and your locale.

Providing graceful movement as well as color, texture, and sound to the landscape, ornamental grasses are versatile and striking.

A Wild Garden

Some of my earliest memories are of searching the woodland for the first wildflowers each spring—hepatica, trillium, bloodroot, Dutchman's breeches, and violets, to name a few. These flowers fascinated me then, and they still do. How can one cease to wonder at the precise mathematics of the three-parted trillium or a flower that could so closely resemble pantaloons on a wash line?

These and other natives of the deciduous oak and maple forests hold a special place in the hearts and imaginations of many gardeners. If you aspire to recreate in your yard a small area that corresponds to this natural habitat, you can, with care and attention to detail.

In the wild, these plants seem to grow with such reckless abandon: whole valleys carpeted in sky blue Virginia bluebells or a hillside golden with downy violets. Yet, many native wildflowers need very specific conditions to grow with any sort of reliability, let alone flourish. Any translation of a wild garden to a cultivated one should be preceded with a study of the trees, shrubs, and flowers that naturally grow together. Observe the type of soil, light, and moisture of the area where you will develop your wild garden.

A spring-blooming woodland wildflower garden demands an area that gets plenty of light during these flowers' main period of growth—early spring. Later, this area should be shaded by trees and shrubs. As would be expected, the soil must be very loose and crumbly, rich with rotted leaves, and able to retain moisture yet be well drained.

Plant List
(number of plants needed in parentheses)

1. Flowering dogwood, *Cornus florida* (1)
2. Shadblow or serviceberry, *Amelanchier laevis* (1)
3. Eastern redbud, *Cercis canadensis* (1)
4. Spicebush, *Lindera Benzoin* (3)
5. Cinnamon fern, *Osmunda cinnamomea* (5)
6. Hay-scented fern, *Dennstaedtia punctilobula* (6)
7. Columbine, *Aquilegia canadensis* (6)
8. Toothed wood fern, *Dryopteris spinulosa* (11)
9. Giant bellwort, *Uvularia grandiflora* (5)
10. Virginia bluebells, *Mertensia virginica* (3)
11. Virginia spiderwort, *Tradescantia virginiana* (3)
12. Blue phlox, *Phlox divaricata* (8)
13. Crested iris, *Iris cristata* (9)
14. Hepatica, *Hepatica americana* or *acutiloba* (3)
15. Shooting-star, *Dodecatheon Meadia* (3)
16. Wintergreen, *Gaultheria procumbens* (9)
17. Wake-robin, *Trillium grandiflorum* (6)
18. Purple trillium, *Trillium erectum* (4)
19. Maidenhair fern, *Adiantum pedatum* (4)
20. Ebony spleenwort, *Aspleni platyneuron* (11)
21. Marginal shield or leather wood fern, *Dryopteris marginalis* (7)
22. Christmas fern, *Polystichum acrostichoides* (6)
23. Jack-in-the-pulpit, *Arisaema triphyllum* (6)
24. Squirrel corn, *Dicentra canadensis* (7)
25. Dutchman's-breeches, *Dicentra Cucullaria* (9)
26. Pink lady's-slipper, *Cypripedium acaule* (3)
27. Yellow lady's-slipper, *Cypripedium Calceolus* var. *pubescens* (3)
28. Foamflower, *Tiarella cordifolia* (14)
29. Downy yellow violet, *Viola pubescens* (8)
30. Spring-beauty, *Claytonia virginica* (5)
31. Bloodroot, *Sanguinaria canadensis* (12)
32. Wild ginger, *Asarum canadense* (12)
33. Solomon's-seal, *Polygonatum biflorum* (7)
34. Sweet white violet, *Viola blanda* (6)

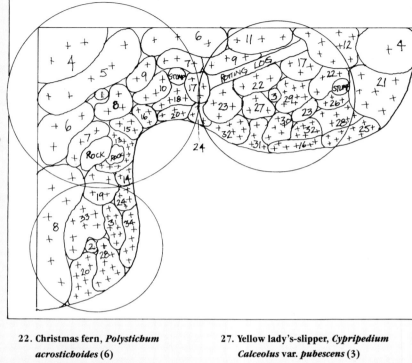

KENNETH SPENGLER

If you have typical construction-site soil, improve it by incorporating leaf mold or peat moss and dehydrated composted manure into the soil. The first summer after planting, mulch around the plants with shredded bark or leaves, and water if rainfall is limited.

Do not try to gather plants from the woods. Instead, purchase nursery-propagated plants from a garden center or mail-order company. Make sure the company does not collect them in the wild. By acting responsibly, we will be able to enjoy flowers growing in their natural state in woodlands for generations to come.

Although the plants suggested here will grow in many areas, you may want to develop a garden of plants that is specific to your area. To do so, study the native habitat and consult books on the wildflowers of your region.

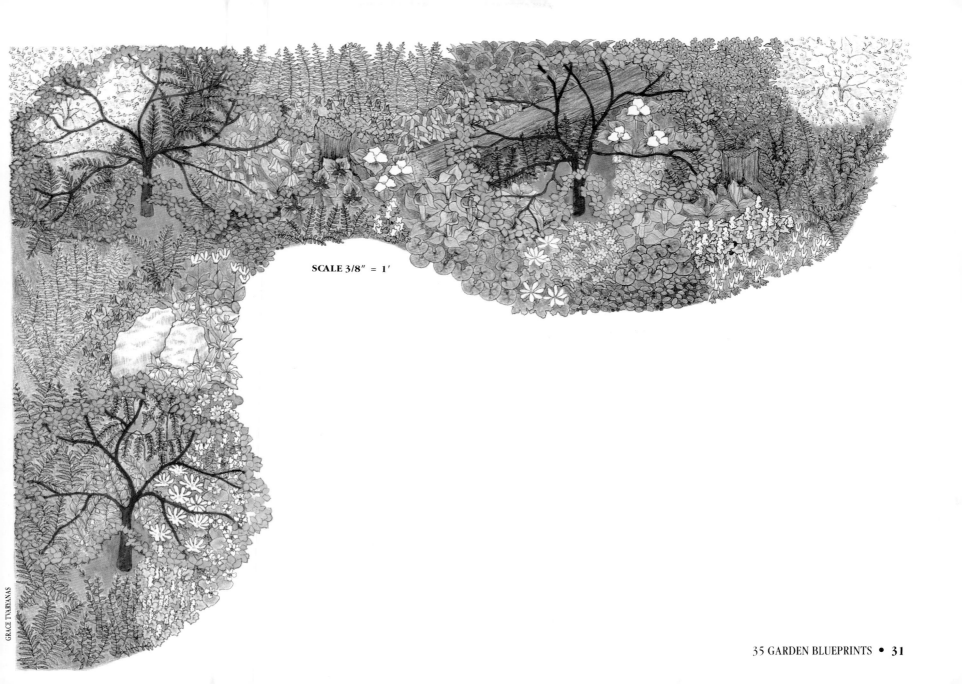

SCALE 3/8″ = 1′

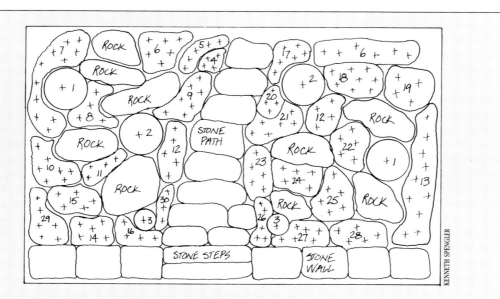

KENNETH SPENGLER

A Rock Garden

Deceptively simple in appearance, a rock garden actually requires a dedicated gardener with a keen sense of ingenuity in order to create a varied, properly proportioned planting that looks natural.

The White Flower Farm catalog has summarized some simple, useful points from H. Lincoln Foster's book, *Rock Gardening: A Guide to Growing Alpines and Other Wildflowers in the American Garden:*

1. The site should be in full sun, never close to a large tree whose roots will soon take over.

2. Use rocks of the neighborhood, for then the artificial outcropping (your rock garden) looks natural. Remember that it's a garden of plants in rocks that is being built, not a garden of assorted rocks.

3. Use large rocks; you may need the help of a contractor to place them. Bury the bottom three-fourths of each.

4. Tilt rocks toward the top of the grade to make the outcropping look more natural and to channel water down to the subsoil.

5. Supply drainage.

6. Soils, which should be deep in the many pockets between the rocks, can be specially prepared to suit plants, but we recommend for beginners one-half part garden loam, one-half part humus, one part of half-inch [1.2 centimeters] crushed rock, and one part of coarse sand.

Plant List
(number of plants needed in parentheses)

1. Dwarf Japanese false cypress, *Chamaecyparis pisifera* Minima (2)

2. American arborvitae, *Thuja occidentalis* 'Tiny Tim' (2)

3. Bird's-nest spruce, *Picea abies* 'Nidiformis' (2)

4. Dwarf bearded iris, *Iris pumila* (4)

5. Mother-of-thyme, *Thymus praecox* or *Serpyllum* 'Coccineus' (5)

6. Cheddar pink, *Dianthus gratianopolitanus* 'Ipswich Crimson' (6)

7. Mountain pink, *Phlox subulata* 'Scarlet Flame' (11)

8. Snow-in-summer, *Cerastium tomentosum* (10)

9. Woolly yarrow, *Achillea tomentosa* (7)

10. English harebell, *Campanula rotundifolia* 'Olympica' (7)

11. Curly chive, *Allium senescens* var. *glaucum* (4)

12. Carpathian harebell, *Campanula carpatica* (9)

13. Siebold stonecrop, *Sedum sieboldii* (10)

14. Candytuft, *Iberis sempervirens* 'Purity' (10)

15. Dwarf blue columbine, *Aquilegia flabellata* (5)

16. Stonecrop, *Sedum spurium* 'Splendens' or 'Dragon's Blood' (4)

17. Crested iris, *Iris cristata* (6)

18. Allwood pink, *Dianthus* x *Allwoodii* (8)

19. Baloon flower, *Platycodon grandiflorus* var. 'Mariesii' (4)

20. Cheddar pink, *Dianthus gratianopolitanus* 'Tiny Rubies' (4)

21. Soapwort, *Saponaria Ocymoides* (6)

22. Columbine, *Aquilegia* x *hybrida* 'Biedermeier' (5)

23. Creeping baby's-breath, *Gypsophila repens* (5)

24. Cranesbill, *Geranium sanguineum* var. *prostratum (lancastsrense)* (5)

25. Wall rock cress, *Arabis caucasica* (6)

26. Thrift, *Armeria maritima* (5)

27. Basket-of-gold, *Aurinia saxatilis* (6)

28. Mountain alyssum, *Alyssum montanum* 'Silver Queen' (5)

29. Pussy-toes, *Antennaria dioica* (3)

30. Purple rock cress, *Aubrieta deltoidea* 'Purple gem' (6)

SCALE 3/16″ = 1′

GRACE TVARVANAS

7. A scree, a heap of fine stones representing a rockslide or the tip of a glacial moraine, used for plants requiring perfect drainage, should be about a foot [30 centimeters] thick, the bottom 3 inches [7.6 centimeters] made to 2- to 3-inch stone [5- to 7.6 centimeters], the "ground" a mixture of half-inch [1.2 centimeters] crushed rock (two parts) and soil (one part).

8. Most rock plants require water in abundance—soak them when the weather supplies less than an inch [2.5 centimeters] of rain a week. Also, it is possible with careful hand-watering to give each plant the amount of water it needs—sedums need less, for example.

9. The size of plant material used depends on the size of the garden. Almost any plant can be used as a rock plant—

the test: how will it look in the composition? Unusual dwarf evergreens are excellent, if planted in pockets restricting their root runs so that they remain dwarf.

The above, admittedly, is oversimplified. But a rock garden is great to work with, particularly if started small and then developed to a point that does not exceed the time the owner can afford to care for it well.

Besides the plants listed, I suggest you interplant with a variety of such hardy, low-growing, spring-blooming bulbs as the species tulips, dwarf daffodils, crocuses, grape hyacinths, dwarf alliums, snowdrops, dwarf anemones, guinea hen flowers, chionodoxas, puschkinias, aconites, and squills. For the end of the growing season, plant the fall-blooming crocuses, colchicums, and the hardy cyclamens.

A Fruit Garden

There is probably no aspect of gardening about which I have such mixed feelings as that of growing fruit. It's a matter of expectations. If you think you're going to grow bushels of blemish-free, grocery-store-type fruit without lifting a finger or a sprayer full of pesticides, then you'll be disappointed. What you will grow is abundant quantities of a wide variety of fruit, including ones that are either impossible or expensive to buy.

For example, when I was growing up, we had one "June" apple tree and another apple of unknown variety. Neither was ever sprayed and, yes, the apples were "wormy." Yet, these two trees produced more apple pies, sauce, jelly, and butter than you can imagine. In addition, I've been able to enjoy such delicacies as fresh strawberries in September, homemade currant jelly, and red raspberry sauce for peach melba.

The fruit garden designed here uses fruit plants instead of the more traditional ornamental trees and shrubs to create a front-yard landscape. Why not have beauty as well as food?

Although many varieties of fruit crops only grow well in certain climates, the ones recommended here are the best possible selections for a wide range of climates, generally producing in southern as well as northern regions. (Gardeners in regions with a winter minimum of 10 degrees F [−12 degrees C] or higher may want to substitute rabbiteye blueberries for the highbush.)

The selections take into consideration the necessary pollination requirements as well. These fruit tree recommendations were made by Ed Fackler of Rocky Meadow Nursery (see

"Sources"), who has grown well over one thousand different varieties of apples, pears, peaches, and plums.

Although no fruit garden is absolutely low maintenance, this one is as close as possible to it. Water the plants regularly and feed them each year in the spring with a complete fertilizer, such as 5–10–10. If you can't live with worms, use a general-purpose fruit tree spray at the manufacturer's recommended rate and schedule for that type of tree. Mulch around all plantings with an organic mulch, such as shredded bark.

The other plants are seldom bothered by pests, except for birds. The blueberries and cherry, in particular, may need to be covered with netting. If you have the time, keep the strawberry runners pinched off to increase fruit production; you'll still get a nice bowlful every week during the summer even if you don't.

Pruning is one of the most important aspects of care, and it is also impossible to adequately describe in this space. My only choice is to recommend that you consult a local specialist or one of the books on fruit gardening. I find the everbearing raspberries are most easily cared for by removing all canes in the spring, which means you'll just get a fall harvest. The elderberries, too, seem to do best if completely cut back—but only every couple of years.

What will really make this garden special is filling in around this basic planting with vegetables, herbs, and flowers. Peppers, tomatoes, lettuce, and bush squash fit in well with the edible landscape. Add your favorite culinary herbs and a variety of annual and perennial flowers for color.

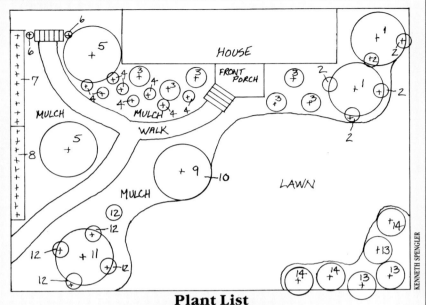

KENNETH SPENGLER

Plant List
(number of plants needed in parentheses)

1. Apple, *Malus sylvestris* 'Scarlet Gayla' and 'Empire' on semidwarfing rootstock (1 of each)
2. Red currant, *Ribes sativum* 'Red Lake' (5)
3. Highbush blueberry, *Vaccinium corymbosum* 'Earliblue,' 'Northland,' 'Blueray,' 'Bluecrop,' 'Berkley,' and 'Jersey' (1 of each)
4. Rhubarb, *Rheum Rhabarbarum* 'Valentine' and 'MacDonald' (4 of each)
5. Pear, *Pyrus communis* 'Harrow Delight' and 'Magness' on semidwarfing rootstock (1 of each)
6. Grape, *Vitis Labrusca* 'Concord' (2)
7. Everbearing red raspberry, *Rubus* 'Heritage' (10)
8. Everbearing yellow raspberry, *Rubus* 'Fallgold' (10)
9. Sour cherry, *Prunus cerasus* 'North Star'
10. Everbearing strawberry, *Fragaria Vescia* 'Tristar' (50)
11. Black haw, *Viburnum prunifolium* (1)
12. Gooseberry, *Ribes uva-crispa* 'Welcome' (5)
13. Highbush cranberry, *Viburnum trilobum* 'Wentworth (3)
14. American elder, *Sambucus canadensis* 'Adams No. 1,' 'Nova,' and 'York' (1 of each)

GRACE TVARYANAS

An English Cottage Garden

A cottage garden is not so much a design as an attitude, a way of life. Therefore, I approach this design for today's gardener with a great deal of misgiving. It is difficult to create the romantic notion that is both the myth and the reality of this type of garden.

However, what we can strive for is that charming informality, that exuberance of spirit that comes from a natural love of plants. In the beginning the English cottage garden was a practical mixture of flowers, herbs, and vegetables. Rural in origin, it ranged in size from postage stamp to well over 1 acre (4047 square meters). There was a backbone of trees and shrubs, and roses were essential.

The cottage garden is very personal. Many of the plants are acquired from friends, acquaintances, and travels, each providing a sentimental link with a person or place. Never expect a cottage garden to be "done." It should be evolving continuously. As English gardener Tony Schilling has written, "I enjoy above all else the constant search for a balanced picture composed of the innumerable forms, textures, habits, and colors of plants."

In keeping with tradition, scatter boxes, feeders, and baths throughout the garden to attract birds. Include the scented plants that attract bees and butterflies. Brightly colored flowers rich with nectar bring hummingbirds to the garden, too.

As your gardening skills and interests increase—and time and funds allow—strive to extend the seasons that your cottage garden has plants in bloom. Some of the traditional English plants for spring flowers that grow well in this country include: primroses, pulmonaria, snowdrops, galanthus, crocus, aconite, species iris and tulips, anemone, dwarf narcissus, and fritillaria. Besides the showy chrysanthemums and asters in the fall, add the dimension of bulbs like cyclamen, colchicum, and fall-blooming crocus.

The English lavender and Merton foxglove used in this design are hardy only through areas with a winter minimum of -20 degrees F (-28 degrees C) or warmer; in colder areas, treat these plants as annuals or substitute other plants. I've used them because they are so much a part of the traditional cottage garden.

Many of the best cottage-style gardens that I have seen have actually been in urban settings, usually around older homes with small lots. The confinement of a small area means every bit of space has been utilized, which creates that exuberant look. Although a cottage garden may look carefree, in reality it demands a great deal of attention. Be sure you are ready for the commitment required. If so, you will be richly rewarded.

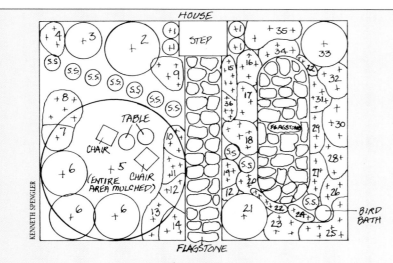

Plant List

(number of plants needed in parentheses)

1. **Climbing rose,** *Rosa* 'Dortmund' (4)
2. **Meyer lilac,** *Syringa Meyeri* 'Palibin' (1)
3. **Rhododendron,** *Rhododendron* 'PJM' (1)
4. **Cranesbill,** *Geranium Endressii* (3)
5. **Allegheny serviceberry,** *Amelanchier laevis* (1)
6. **Red currant,** *Ribes sativum* 'Red Lake' (3)
7. **Rhubarb,** *Rheum Rhabarbarum* 'Valentine' (1)
8. **Cornflower,** *Centaurea Cyanus* 'Jubilee Gem' (6)
9. **Lady's-mantle,** *Alchemilla vulgaris* (4)
10. **English harebell,** *Campanula rotundifolia* 'Olympica' (4)
11. **Flowering tobacco,** *Nicotiana alata* 'Nicki White' (4)
12. **Balloon flower,** *Platycodon grandiflorus* (4)
13. **French sorrel,** *Rumex scutatus* (3)
14. **Pineapple-scented sage,** *Salvia rutilans* (3)
15. **Cottage pink,** *Dianthus deltoides* 'Doris' (5)
16. **Threadleaf coreopis,** *Coreopsis verticillata* 'Moonbeam' (3)
17. **Merton foxglove,** *Digitalis* x *mertonensis* (3)
18. **Speedwell,** *Veronica spicata* 'Icicle' (5)
19. **Hyssop,** *Hyssopus officinalis* (2)
20. **Miniature rose,** *Rosa* 'Old Glory' (3)
21. **Rugosa rose,** *Rosa rugosa* 'Blanc Double de Coubert' (1)
22. **Treasure flower,** *Gazania splendens* 'Mini-Star' (10)
23. **Cosmos,** *Cosmos bipinnatus* 'Sensation Mixed' (4)
24. **Clustered bellflower,** *Campanula glomerata* 'Superba' (3)
25. **Hollyhock,** *Alcea rosea* 'Pinafore' (7)
26. **Borage,** *Borago officinalis* (3)
27. **Shasta daisy,** *Chrysanthemum maximum* 'Alaska' (4)
28. **Monkshood,** *Aconitum Carmichaelii* (3)
29. **Yarrow,** *Achillea taygetea* 'Moonshine' (3)
30. **Gas plant,** *Dictamnus albus* (3)
31. **Iceland poppy,** *Papaver nudicaule* 'Sparkling Bubbles Mixed' or 'Wonderland Mixed' (5)
32. **Siberian larkspur,** *Delphinium grandiflorum* 'Connecticut Yankees' (3)
33. **Golden elder,** *Sambucus racemosa* 'Plumosa Aurea' (1)
34. **English lavender,** *Lavandula angustifolia* 'Munstead' (3)
35. **Pincushion flower,** *Scabiosa caucasica* (5)
36. **Lamb's-ears,** *Stachys byzantina* (4)

GRACE TVARANAS

SCALE 5/32″ = 1′

ANNE MESKEY

A Formal English Garden

English country estate gardens are actually composed of many small gardens situated on a large property. Needless to say, they are maintained by a staff of gardeners. If you have the requisite property and money, you'll need more than this book to develop your site. An interpretation of this style of gardening is feasible, however, on a much smaller scale and can be appropriate for a wide range of houses and settings.

This type of British garden combines a romantic view of the natural landscape with an ordered formality. Within the severeness of walls, hedges, and symmetrical geometric beds is a profusion of flowers, or, additionally, vistas encompass broad sweeps of trees, shrubs, and fields. To appreciate the patterns created in the formal areas, this part of the garden is best created at a level that is below the point from which it is most often viewed, say a living room or terrace.

The garden created here is adapted from the one at Abbotswood in the Cotswold hills designed by Gertrude Jekyll. Although small in scale, it combines the traditional elements of formal beds, flowers, a hedge, geometrical evergreens, plus trees, shrubs, and roses. What is not traditional is that this is actually a relatively low-maintenance garden. Relative is the key word here; some regular care is involved but much less than would be expected.

For example, the juniper hedge is intended to be grown naturally rather than typically sheared. The dwarf spruces have a clipped appearance without a pair of shears ever coming close. Even the chore of periodic edging of the beds can be minimized by using brick or other edging material.

The roses are excellent new hybrids of unu-

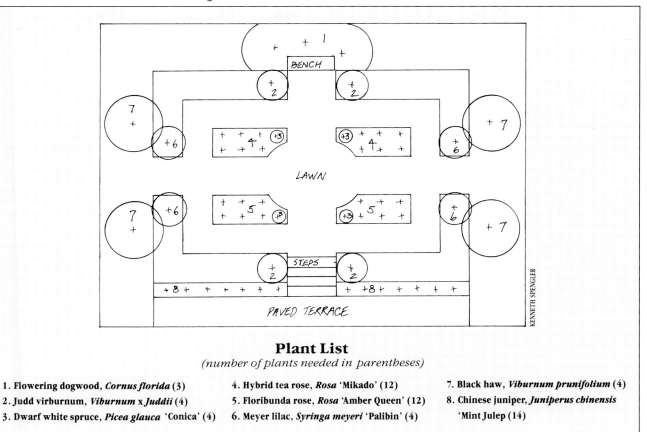

KENNETH SPENGLER

Plant List
(number of plants needed in parentheses)

1. Flowering dogwood, *Cornus florida* (3)
2. Judd virburnum, *Viburnum* x *Juddii* (4)
3. Dwarf white spruce, *Picea glauca* 'Conica' (4)

4. Hybrid tea rose, *Rosa* 'Mikado' (12)
5. Floribunda rose, *Rosa* 'Amber Queen' (12)
6. Meyer lilac, *Syringa meyeri* 'Palibin' (4)

7. Black haw, *Viburnum prunifolium* (4)
8. Chinese juniper, *Juniperus chinensis* 'Mint Julep' (14)

sual color and form. The floribunda 'Amber Queen' is exceptionally fragrant; 'Mikado' bears flowers when younger and in more quantity than almost any other hybrid tea rose. To simplify maintenance, use an all-purpose systemic fertilizer-pesticide.

I envision this garden in a backyard, just below a stone terrace, with a tree-and-shrub bor-

der at a distance surrounding the edge of the lot and a perfectly maintained lawn. The four outermost beds can be planted with any combination of annuals, perennials, and bulbs that you desire. For ideas, see "An Annual and Perennial Garden," (page 27).

An added English touch would be to surround the four innermost beds with such an

edging as *Ageratum* 'Blue Danube,' germander, or dwarf boxwood. *Viburnum* x *Burkwoodii, V.* x *carlcephalum,* or *V. Carlesii* can be substituted for the judd viburnum. Although sometimes considered a shrub, in this setting you should grow the edible-fruited black haw as a small tree by training it to a single trunk.

A Victorian Garden

Whether small and simple or large and ornate, there is a wealth of wonderful Victorian-era homes in our cities, small towns, and rural areas. As more and more people become involved in restoring these houses, there is a concurrent interest in the gardening of that period.

The present-day ubiquitous foundation planting of evergreens has its origins in the nineteenth century. Many of the Victorian homes were set on high foundations, and shrubs served to cover up, soften, insulate, and provide a visual "connection" with the surrounding yard. You might see junipers, boxwood, azaleas, rhododendrons, false cypress, chamaecyparis, yew, nandina, or pittosporum used for this purpose.

Deciduous shrubs, or those that lose their leaves in the winter, were also incorporated in the foundation plantings and in borders at the edge of the yard. Some of the old-fashioned favorites include lilac, mock orange, hydrangea, spiraea, and rose-of-Sharon. Large evergreen and deciduous trees shaded the high porches that were often on all three sides of a house. Evergreen or perennial ground covers and edging plants grew under the trees and shrubs or bordered the walks.

The jewel in this setting was usually one or more beds of brightly colored flowers or foliage. The formal annual garden in this book is an example of this style. These beds were inspired by the French parterre, often with flowing, intricate shapes. Spring-blooming tulips would give way to dahlias, cannas, caladiums, impatiens, geraniums, scarlet sage, wax begonias, or coleus.

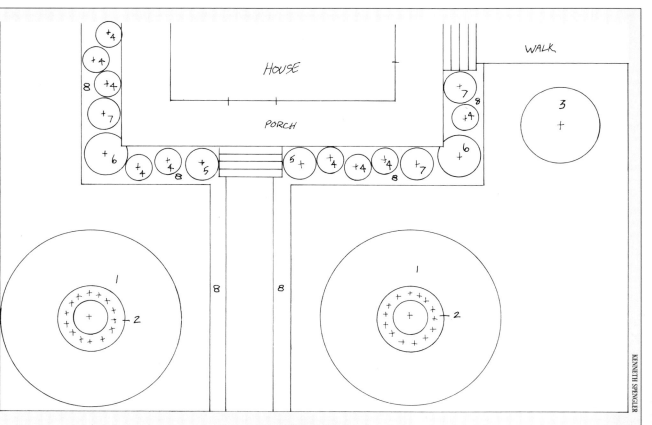

KENNETH SPENGLER

Plant List
(number of plants needed in parentheses)

1. Norway maple, *Acer platanoides* 'Crimson King' (2)

2. English ivy, *Hedera Helix* 'Wilsonii' (28)

3. Peegee hydrangea, *Hydrangea paniculata* 'Grandiflora' (1)

4. Chinese juniper, *Juniperus chinensis* 'Mint Julep' (9)

5. Summer-sweet, *Clethra alnifolia* 'Pinkspire' (2)

6. Sweet azalea, *Rhododendron arborescens* (2)

7. Hicks yew, *Taxus x media* 'Hicksii' (3)

8. Caladium and impatiens, Fancy-leaved *Caladium* x *hortulanum* 'Mixed' and *Impatiens Wallerana* 'Accent Pink' (40 of each, alternately planted along front walk and in front of shrubs)

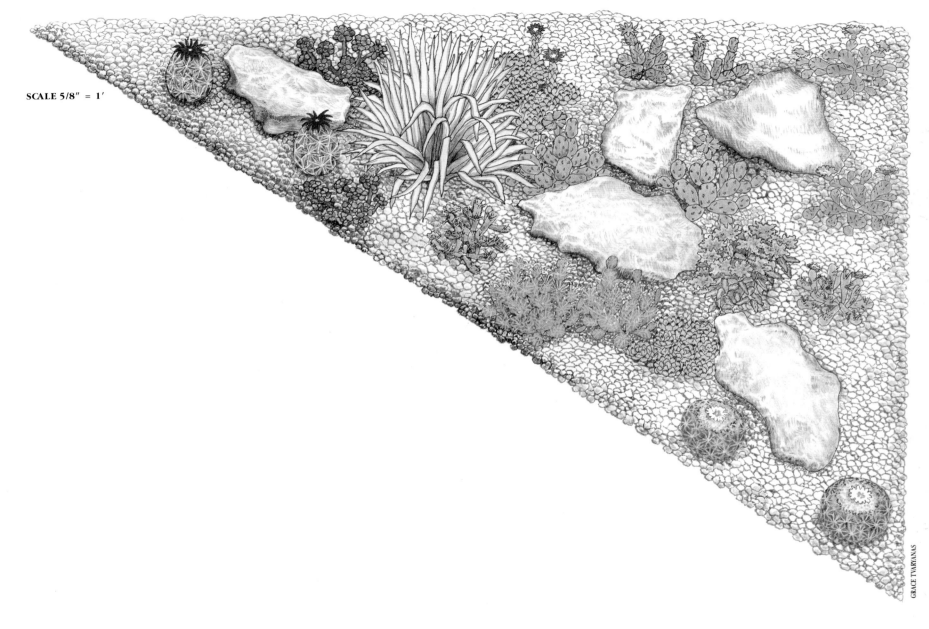

SCALE 5/8″ = 1′

A Cacti and Succulent Garden

Why would you go to the trouble necessary to have a desert garden if you don't live in a desert climate? Perhaps because your house is in the style of the Texas hill country or maybe it's a log cabin or made of stucco with a tile roof. Then again, perhaps you're fascinated by cacti and succulents.

Whatever your reasons, there are several ways to have at least a part of your yard done in a style reminiscent of the Southwest. One is by sinking pots of cacti and succulents into the soil, then taking them indoors during the winter. Another is to place tubs of cacti and succulents on your patio, terrace, or about the yard, and, again, take them indoors in winter.

A third way is to use cacti and succulents that are hardy. According to John Sabuco in *The Best of the Hardiest* there are at least thirteen varieties of cacti that have ornamental value and are hardy to –20 degrees F (–28 degrees C) or colder. To meet the requirements of this book, or a minimum temperature of –30 degrees F (–34 degrees C), our list is shortened only by five. For hardy succulents, the gardener can look to the sedums and sempervivums. Most of the sempervivums, or "live forevers" are hardy only to –20 degrees F (–28 degrees C), but many of the sedums, or "stonecrops," are hardy to –40 degrees F (–40 degrees C).

Since there are so few and they are basically not very large, I have chosen to make this a rather small garden that is given a place of honor in the yard, such as near a front door or outdoor living space. You may want to consider putting your cacti and succulent garden in a raised bed.

Even where the climate is ideal, a cacti and succulent garden is not easy to create or maintain. A garden of this type in the Southwest must be constantly thinned and pruned. In other climate zones, the key is plant selection and soil preparation. To combat the high humidity, ample rainfall, and withering winter winds, cacti and succulents must have soil that is absolutely fast draining. Use a naturally sloping area or create one.

The Time-Life Encyclopedia of Gardening volume on cacti and succulents suggests the following procedure. Remove the soil in a sunny area to a depth of 6 inches (15 centimeters). Add a pile of limestone rocks or broken bricks about 1 foot (30 centimeters) high. The sloping sides ensure fast drainage. Add a 2-inch (5-centimeter) layer of gravel and a 1-inch (2.5-centimeter) layer of sand. Finally, cover the bed with 6 to 8 inches (15 to 20 centimeters) of a soil mixture composed of one part topsoil, one part leaf mold, one part gravel, and two parts sand. Add .5 cup (.23 liters) of bonemeal to each gallon (4.5 liters) of planting mix.

Mulch with pebbles, which will reflect heat to the plants and keep their bases dry. Feed plants throughout the growing season with a fertilizer such as 5–10–10 at the manufacturer's recommended rate.

Plant List
(number of plants needed in parentheses)

1. Adam's-needle, *Yucca filamentosa* 'Golden Sword' (1)
2. Aizoon stonecrop, *Sedum Aizoon* (1)
3. Spiny star, *Coryphantha vivipara* (2)
4. Prickly pear, *Opuntia bumifusa* var. *austrina (compressa)* (2)
5. Utah grizzly-bear opuntia, *Opuntia erinacea* var. *utabensis* (2)
6. Pigmy tuna, *Opuntia fragilis* (2)
7. Plains prickly pear, *Opuntia polyacantha* (2)
8. Whipple opuntia, *Opuntia Whipplei* (2)
9. Snowball cactus, *Pediocactus Simpsonii* (2)
10. Oregon stonecrop, *Sedum oreganum* (2)
11. Hen-and-chickens, *Sempervivum tectorum* (2)

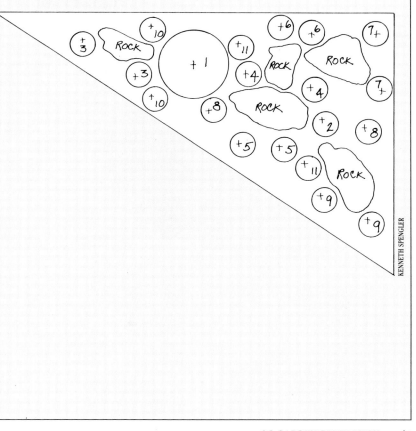

KENNETH SPENGLER

A Low Maintenance Garden

More often than I care to admit, it seems that the term "low-maintenance gardening" lies somewhere between misnomer and oxymoron. For just like kids and pets, plants are living entities and require tender, loving care. Needless to say, some must have more than others.

The advantage of plants over children and animals is that you can choose your odds with a relatively large margin of reliability. By combining a little bit of book and magazine study with conversation with people who have gardening experience, you can choose plants that have a good low-maintenance track record, are tolerant of a wide range of soils, can withstand some drought, require little maintenance, have few pests, and are also attractive much of the year.

The other aspect of gardening that can make it low maintenance is mechanical. By using mulches, perhaps one of stone or an organic material, such as shredded bark, either alone or in combination with fabric, you eliminate the problem of weeds. Mulches also help in slowing down moisture evaporation, thus reducing the need for watering. Mowing strips and drip irrigation systems are other examples of materials that make gardening life easier.

A popular way to simplify the landscape as well as gardening chores is by eliminating as much of the lawn as possible, using ground covers instead. The term "ground cover" generally refers to a broad group of plants that are perennial, sometimes evergreen, trailing or clumping, and less than 1 foot (30 centimeters) tall. Some of the ground covers you may be familiar with are English ivy, pachysandra, aegopodium, ajuga, arctostaphylos, cotoneaster, hosta, hypericum, creeping juniper, and vinca.

An effective low-maintenance garden that uses ground covers requires considerable time and money at the beginning, but once established it needs much less upkeep than one that uses other plants. The keys to success include choosing plants suited to your region and garden; knowing before starting that you can meet the plant's cultural requirements; preparing the soil well with organic supplements before planting; watering regularly the first year; and mulching to keep weeds under control.

The plants listed grow well in many of the climate zones, and for the plan shown you can choose from among any of these. The extreme south and southwest parts of the United States require different plants. I suggest consulting with a very reliable local nursery.

GRACE TVARANAS

Plant List
(number of plants needed in parentheses)

1. River birch, *Betula nigra* 'Heritage' (1)
2. Lace-bark pine, *Pinus Bungeana* (1)
3. Cinnamon fern, *Osmunda cinnamomea* (3)
4. Ground cover of your choice

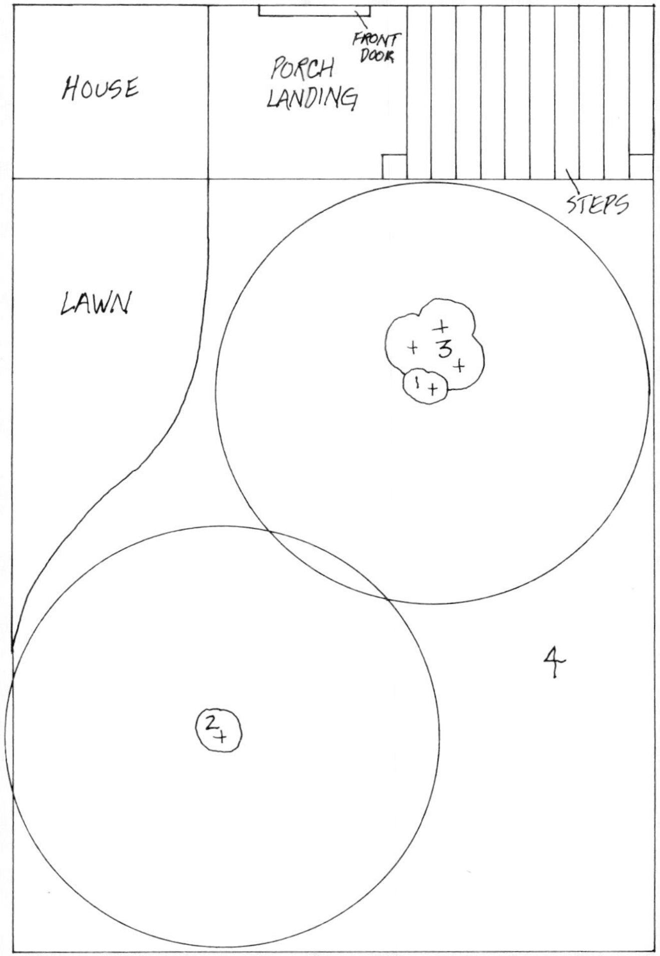

HOUSE

PORCH LANDING

FRONT DOOR

STEPS

LAWN

+
+ 3 +
1 +

4

2 +

KENNETH SPENGLER

An Everlastings Garden

Beautifully crafted bouquets, wreaths, ornaments, and other dried-flower decorations are a lovely way to naturally enhance the home environment. Although just about any flower can be dried using sand or silica gel, there are certain ones that retain their shape and color with much less effort. Most need only to be hung upside down in a dark, airy place for a week or so; others dry right on the plant. These readily dried types of flowers are called everlastings.

Many of these everlastings are annuals—that is, they grow, flower, and die in one season. They should be harvested just as they come into bloom. For this reason, they are grown in an area much like the one in which a traditional vegetable garden thrives closed off from the rest of the garden by a tall fence. Not only have flowers been included in this area but also brilliantly colored Indian corn and miniature gourds, wonderfully feathery annual grasses, and plants with unusual pods and seeds, such as unicorn and money plants and love-in-a-mist. The rest of the garden is a fairly traditional design, utilizing a mixed border of trees, shrubs, and perennials surrounding a lawn. A patio adjacent to the house is partly covered with an arbor. What is not traditional is the choice of plant material. Each one has been selected because it has some aspect that is useful in dried arrangements and crafts, be it branches, berries, pods, leaves, or flowers. All of these elements, except the leaves, can be used by simply air drying.

The leaves of the hawthorn, rhododendron, smokebush, siebold viburnum, and toothed wood fern can be preserved in a mixture of one part glycerin with two parts hot water. Put the base of the branches or fronds into a tall jar filled with the mixture just as you would a bouquet. Over the next several weeks the glycerin will be absorbed and the leaves will darken but remain pliable. Remove them from the glycerin mixture and store them in boxes or jars.

(continued on next page)

ANNE MESKEY

Plant List
(number of plants needed in parentheses)

1. Washington hawthorn, *Crataegus Phaenopyrum* (1)
2. Winterberry, *Ilex verticillata* 'Winter Red' (4)
3. Rhododendron, *Rhododendron* 'PJM.' (3)
4. Purple-leaved smokebush, *Cotinus Coggygria* 'Royal Purple' (1)
5. Siebold viburnum, *Viburnum Sieboldii* (1)
6. Pussy willow, *Salix discolor* (1)
7. Japanese fan-tail willow, *Salix sachalinensis* 'Sekko' (1)
8. Grape, *Vitis Labrusca* 'Concord' (3)
9. Harry Lauder's walking stick, *Corylus Avellana* 'Contorta' (1)
10. Smooth hydrangea, *Hydrangea arborescens* 'Grandiflora' or 'Annabelle' (2)
11. Oriental bittersweet, *Celastrus orbiculatus* (2)
12. Shrub rose, *Rosa* 'Bonica' (6)
13. Corkscrew willow, *Salix, Matsudana* 'Tortuosa' (1)
14. Winterberry, *Ilex verticillata* (male pollinator) (1)
15. Eulalia, *Miscanthus sinensis* 'Gracillimus' (4)
16. Yarrow, *Achillea taygetea* 'Moonshine' (6)
17. Baby's-breath, *Gypsophila paniculata* 'Bristol Fairy' (3)
18. Everlasting, *Anaphalis triplinervis* (3)
19. Lamb's-ears, *Stachys byzantina* (3)
20. Chinese lantern, *Physalis Alkekengi* (3) (perennial in areas with −30 degrees F [−34 degrees C] or warmer winter minimum; otherwise grow as an annual)

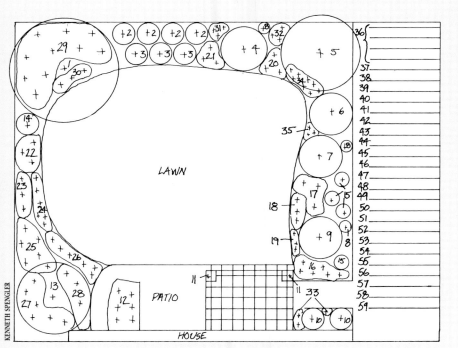

21. Yarrow, *Achillea filipendulina* 'Coronation Gold' (3)
22. Globe thistle, *Echinops Ritro* (3)
23. Monkshood, *Aconitum Carmichaelii* (3)
24. Sea lavender, *Limonium latifolium* (6)
25. Common wormwood, *Artemesia Absinthium* 'Lambrook Silver' (6)
26. German statice, *Goniolimon tataricum* (also listed as *Limonium tataricum)* (6)
27. Silver-king artemisia, *Artemesia ludoviciana* var. *albula* (6)
28. Toothed wood fern, *Dryopteris spinulosa* (5)
29. Ostrich fern, *Matteuccia Struthiopteris* (10)
30. Sea holly, *Eryngium alpinum* (3)
31. Globe onion, *Allium aflatunense* (3)
32. Giant globe onion, *Allium giganteum* (3)
33. Showy sedum, *Sedum spectabile* 'Autumn Joy' (3)
34. Coralbells, *Heuchera sanguinea* (7)
35. Garlic chive, *Allium tuberosum* (3)
36. Indian corn, *Zea Mays* 'Rainbow' and miniature Indian corn, *Zea Mays* 'Cutie Pops,' 'Pretty Pops,' or 'Symphonie' (2 rows of each); interplant corn with gourd, *Cucurbita* 'Small Gourds Mixed' and miniature pumpkin, *Cucurbita* 'Jack-Be-Little' or 'Sweetie Pie' (4 plants of each)
37. Okra, *Abelmoschus esculentus* 'Clemson Spineless' and 'Burgundy' (1 packet of each)
38. Unicorn plant, *Proboscidea louisianica* (1 packet)
39. Money plant, *Lunaria annua* (1 packet)
40. Big quaking grass, *Briza maxima* (1 packet)
41. Hare's-tail grass, *Lagurus ovatus* (1 packet)
42. Foxtail millet, *Setaria italica* (1 packet)
43. Job's-tears, *Coix Lacryma-Jobi* (1 packet)
44. Winged everlasting, *Ammobium alatum* (1 packet)
45. Acrolinum, *Helipterum roseum* (1 packet)
46. Immortelle, *Xeranthemum annuum* (1 packet)
47. Bells-of-Ireland, *Moluccella laevis* (1 packet)
48. Cockscomb, *Celosia cristata* 'Floradale Mixed' (1 packet)
49. Cockscomb, *Celosia cristata* 'Apricot Brandy' (1 packet)
50. Cockscomb, *Celosia cristata* 'Century Mixed' (1 packet)
51. Love-in-a-mist, *Nigella damascena* 'Persian Jewels Mixed' (1 packet)
52. Statice, *Limonium sinuatum* 'Mixed Art Shades' (1 packet)
53. Statice, *Limonium sinuatum* 'Mixed' (1 packet)
54. Globe amaranth, *Gomphrena globosa* 'Strawberry Fields' (1 packet)
55. Globe amaranth, *Gomphrena globosa* 'Mixed' (1 packet)
56. Strawflower, *Helichrysum bracteatum* 'Park's Pasel Mix' (1 packet)
57. Strawflower, *Helichrysum bracteatum* 'Bright Bikinis' (1 packet)
58. Rocket larkspur, *Consolida ambigua* 'Giant Imperial Mixture' (1 packet) (also listed as *Delphinium ajacis*)
59. Mealy-cup sage, *Salvia farinacea* 'Victoria' (1 packet)

A Dry Garden

If you live in an area that doesn't receive much rainfall or have a garden with fast-draining soil or other conditions that make the soil particularly dry, don't give up on creating a garden. Consider creating a dry landscape, or *xeriscape,* composed of plants that are adaptable to dry growing conditions. By drawing upon plants from the various arid regions of the world, you can have a landscape that is varied and interesting.

The trees and shrubs chosen for this backyard offer texture and color throughout the seasons with minimal care. The three hedges of upright glossy buckthorn, mentor barberry, and shrubby cinquefoil need no special pruning, yet they screen unsightly views, provide a windbreak, and create a feeling of privacy.

Growing 10 to 12 feet (3 to 3.6 meters) tall, the buckthorn has dark, glossy foliage and a bonus of inconspicuous flowers that produce berries which in turn attract birds. The small, leathery leaves of the 5-foot (1.5-meter) tall mentor barberry are a very dark green; in northern areas, they'll fall off by the holiday season, but in warmer areas, they are evergreen. The shrubby cinquefoil recommended here grows about 2.5 feet (76 centimeters) tall, has finely divided foliage, and bears 2-inch (5-centimeter) golden yellow flowers during most of the summer.

The accent tree for the patio is a small maple with vivid red fall color; it usually has multiple stems. The architectural lines at the corner of the house are softened with a large shrubby tamarisk, with its feathery blue-green foliage

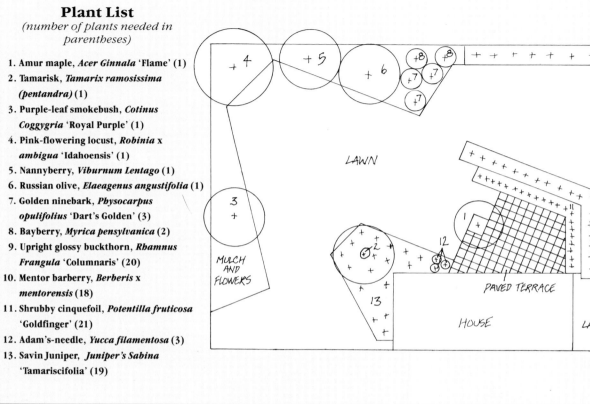

Plant List
(number of plants needed in parentheses)

1. Amur maple, *Acer Ginnala* 'Flame' (1)
2. Tamarisk, *Tamarix ramosissima (pentandra)* (1)
3. Purple-leaf smokebush, *Cotinus Coggygria* 'Royal Purple' (1)
4. Pink-flowering locust, *Robinia* x *ambigua* 'Idahoensis' (1)
5. Nannyberry, *Viburnum Lentago* (1)
6. Russian olive, *Elaeagenus angustifolia* (1)
7. Golden ninebark, *Physocarpus opulifolius* 'Dart's Golden' (3)
8. Bayberry, *Myrica pensylvanica* (2)
9. Upright glossy buckthorn, *Rhamnus Frangula* 'Columnaris' (20)
10. Mentor barberry, *Berberis* x *mentorensis* (18)
11. Shrubby cinquefoil, *Potentilla fruticosa* 'Goldfinger' (21)
12. Adam's-needle, *Yucca filamentosa* (3)
13. Savin Juniper, *Juniper's Sabina* 'Tamariscifolia' (19)

and plumes of pink flowers. The softness is repeated underneath with Savin juniper acting as a ground cover. The swordlike leaves of the three yuccas provide a bold contrast. Once established, the yucca will bear tall spikes of white bell-shaped flowers in summer.

The shrub-and-tree border in the other corner of the yard continues the diagonal design. The plants chosen for this area also have a variety of foliage colors and textures and flower during different seasons; several have berries that again attract birds to the garden.

Although all of these plants are very tolerant of dry soils, it is still important that you water and mulch them when they are newly planted. Use a fabric mulch covered with bark chips or bark chips alone. Either way, this helps plants establish themselves, conserves moisture, and keeps weeds at a minimum.

A lawn is one of the worst offenders when it comes to water usage, but the newer types of slow-growing fescues perform best with little water or fertilizer. Some of these include 'Spartan,' 'Reliant,' 'Waldina,' 'Scaldis,' 'Rebel,' and 'Falcon.' An alternative is to include one of the new ryegrass varieties like 'Manhattan II' in your bluegrass lawn. In southern areas, try sodding with 'Tifway' Bermuda grass.

Neither must you give up annual and perennial flowers in a dry landscape. The number and diversity of plants that you can use is virtually limitless. Use whatever combination you prefer in the large, angular bed around the trees and shrubs. Or, just leave the beds unplanted but mulched for a simpler look as well as less maintenance.

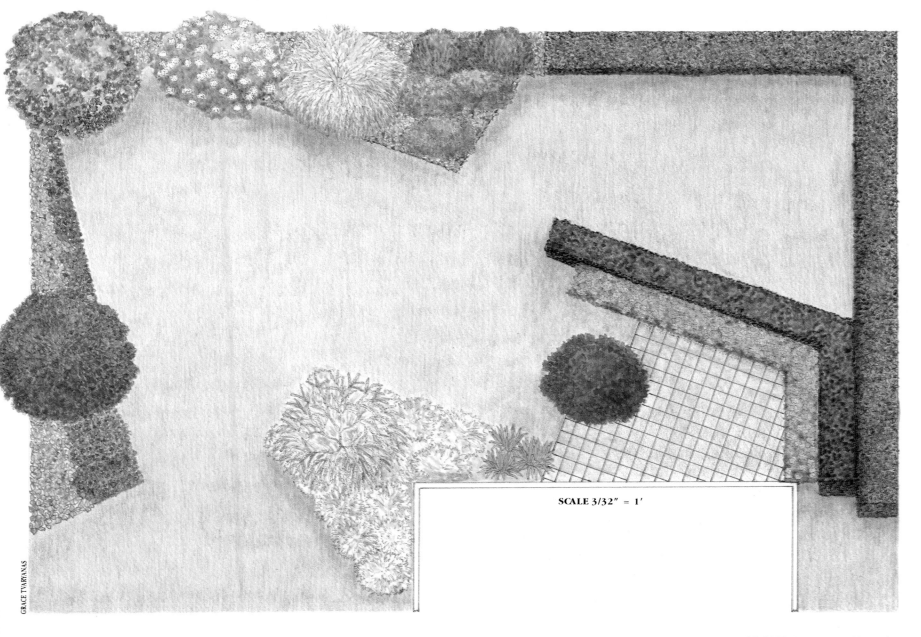

SCALE 3/32″ = 1′

GRACE TVARYANAS

A Water Garden

No other aspect of gardening has quite the attraction as a pool of water, floating leaves, and dazzling water-lily blossoms. At one time, water gardens were strictly the domain of the wealthy or determined, but new means of construction and maintenance plus improved plants have changed all that. A water garden is quite feasible for any home owner now.

A water garden can be as small as half a whiskey barrel or as large as a lake. Where concrete was once the only option for creating a pool, now there are sheets of PVC or fiberglass forms to line the pool.

At least six hours of full sun a day are necessary for most water plants to bloom. Keep them away from trees and shrubs that drop their leaves, as these create a maintenance nightmare. Other considerations include access to water for filling the pool, electricity for pumps or lights, and a relatively flat area.

The size and shape of your water garden should be compatible with the rest of the landscape. An irregular, informal shape will blend in well with a naturalistic landscape with curving lines. A more formally shaped pool, such as a rectangle, square, circle, or oval, will be the perfect accent to a garden with similar formal lines.

Water gardens can be installed anytime during the growing season up to thirty days before the first fall frost. Before digging your pool, purchase the liner you prefer; PVC sheets are less expensive than the fiberglass forms but don't last as long. Send for the water garden catalogs listed in this book, and choose what's best for you. Check local zoning boards for regulations concerning pools.

Excavate the soil to the depth of the pool form or about 1.5 feet (45 centimeters) if using a PVC liner; remove any sticks or stones that could damage the liner. For the pool shown, cut a shelf into two sides at 9 to 10 inches (22 to 25 centimeters) for shallow water plants. Check to see that the top of the pool is level. To protect the liner, line the hole with a .5 inch (1.2 centimeters) of sand or carpet remnants. If using PVC, carefully press it into the contours of the pool, fill the pond with water, then trim the edges to within 1 foot (30 centimeters) of the pool. Camouflage the edges of the pool with flagstone, as shown, concrete pavers, or whatever you prefer, preferably set in reinforced mortar.

There are three main types of aquatic plants: *submerged, floating leaved,* and *emergent.* Submerged plants provide hiding places for fish, frogs, and snails and help to keep algae growth in check. Plant them in small pots of soil covered with a layer of gravel.

Floating-leaved plants, most notably the water lilies, provide glamour in the pool. There are both hardy and tropical types. Plant them in tubs of soil covered with gravel. Place them so that their surface is about 10 inches (25 centimeters) below the water's surface.

The roots of emergent, or bog, plants are in water and the leaves and flowers lie above the water. They are set in larger pots of soil with a gravel surface.

The mail-order catalogs from water garden companies provide a wealth of information on designing pools as well as how to grow and care for aquatic plants. They also supply fish for your pool. There are many excellent books on water gardening, but one of particular note is *Water Gardens for Plants and Fish* by Charles Thomas.

Plant List
(number of plants needed in parentheses)

1. Hardy water lily, *Nymphaea* 'Fabiola' (1)
2. Hardy water lily, *Nymphaea odorata* 'Sulfurea Grandiflora' (1)
3. Blue flag, *Iris versicolor* (1)
4. Siberian iris, *Iris sibirica* (1)
5. Yellow water iris, *Iris Pseudacorus* (1)
6. Lizard's-tail, *Saururus cernuus* (1)
7. Common horsetail, *Equisetum byemale* (1)
8. Pickerel rush, *Pontederia cordata* (1)
9. Bogbean, *Menyanthes trifoliata* (2)
10. Anacharis, *Elodea canadensis* var. *gigantea* (4)
11. Awl-leaf arrowhead, *Sagittaria subulata* (4)
12. Water celery, *Vallisneria americana* (4)
13. Milfoil, *Myriophyllum a...*
14. Fanwort, *Cabomba caro... a* (3)

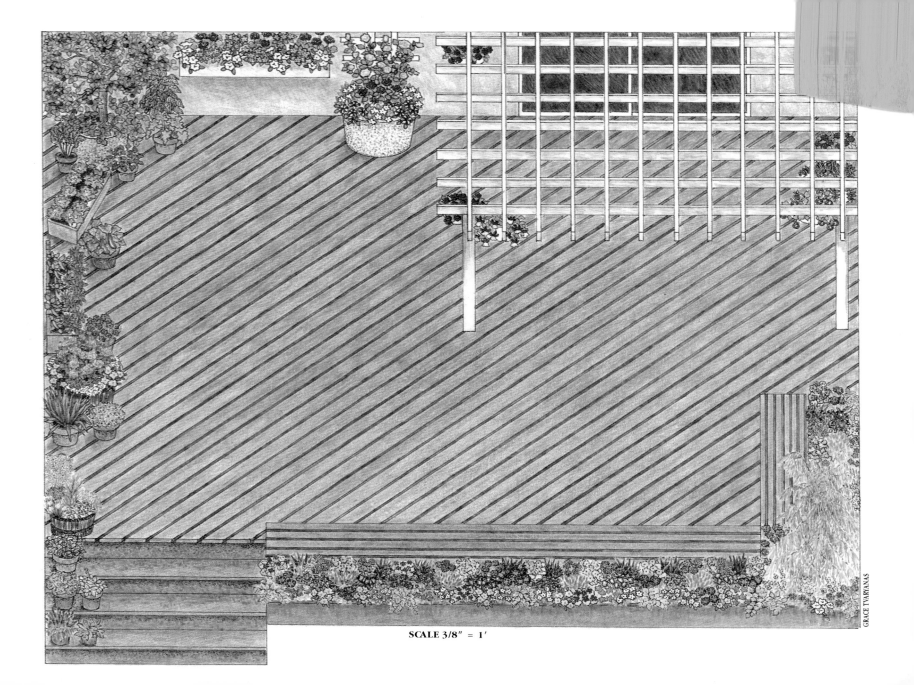

SCALE 3/8″ = 1′

GRACE TVARVANAS

A Container Garden

When I was growing up, the closest anyone I knew came to gardening in containers was a pot of geraniums on the back steps. Today, container gardening is considerably more. In fact, you can have the entire range of plants in containers just as in a ''regular'' landscape, including trees, shrubs, roses, annual and perennial flowers, bulbs, fruits, vegetables, and herbs.

There are several factors necessary for successfully gardening in containers. These entail meeting the plants' needs in terms of soil, drainage, fertilizer, water, and light.

For most people, the simplest solution to soil is actually what's called a ''soilless potting mix.'' This is a combination of sphagnum peat moss, perlite and/or vermiculite, as well as fertilizer. If you're doing a lot of container gardening but don't want to mix your own, it is most economical to buy it in 50-pound (18-kilogram) bags. A soilless mixture is preferable to garden soil because it weighs less and drains better. Besides having a potting mix that drains well, the containers used should have several drainage holes and a layer of gravel at the bottom.

Because the amount of ''soil'' is limited in containers, having adequate nutrition available is crucial. In addition to the fertilizer in the potting mix, I feed at least every two weeks during the growing season with a water-soluble plant food. You can also use a once-a-season, slow-release type of fertilizer, applying at the manufacturer's recommendation.

Providing adequate moisture is crucial to container gardening success. During the height of summer heat, watering at least once a day will probably be necessary. When planning your container garden, make sure a source of water is readily available. It's easiest to use a hose with a ''soaker'' end so that the water comes out gently, not in a blast. You might also want to consider a drip irrigation system designed for container gardening or a sprinkler system.

Choose plants for your container garden just as you would for any landscape. Plants that need full sun when grown in the ground will need the same amount in containers and vice versa for shade-loving plants.

Another key to a spectacular container garden is to space plants so that it seems like you're overplanting. As plants mature, the lush effect will be glorious. Plenty of water and an ample amount of fertilizer are also crucial.

The container garden shown is sited on a large deck complete with a trellised area and built-in benches and planters. The other containers can be made up of a variety of tubs, barrels, and pots in wood, plastic, clay, or fiberglass, depending on your preferences and budget.

Plant List
(number of plants needed in parentheses)

HANGING BASKETS

1. Fuchsia, *Fuchsia* x *hybrida* 'Swingtime' (2)
2. Impatiens, *Impatiens Wallerana* 'Futura Red' (3 baskets with 3 plants each)
3. Dallas fern, *Nephrolepis exaltata* 'Dallas' (1)
4. Tomato, *Lycopersicon Lycopersicum* 'Basket King' (1)

BENCH PLANTERS

1. Variegated annual vinca, *Vinca major* 'Variegata' (7)
2. Mealy-cup sage, *Salvia farinacea* 'Victoria' (5)
3. French marigold, *Tagetes patula* 'Queen Sophia' (9)
4. French marigold, *Tagetes patula* 'Janie Flame' (10)
5. Tomato, *Lycopersicon Lycopersicum* 'Pixie II' (5)
6. Sweet pepper, *Capsicum annuum* 'Park's Pot' (5)
7. Common garden petunia, *Petunia* x *hybrida* 'Yellow Magic' (8)
8. Garden nasturtium, *Tropaeolum majus* 'Whirlybird Mixed' (14)
9. Ornamental pepper, *Capsicum annuum* 'Holiday Flame' (11)
10. Italian bellflower, *Campanula isophylla* 'Stella Blue' (6)
11. Flowering tobacco, *Nicotiana alata* 'Nicki White' (6)

(continued on next page)

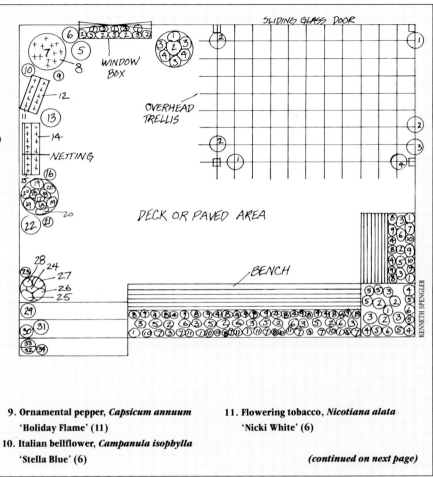

SLIDING GLASS DOOR

WINDOW BOX

OVERHEAD TRELLIS

NETTING

DECK OR PAVED AREA

BENCH

KENNETH SPENGLER

SQUARE CORNER PLANTER

1. Weeping western cedar, *Juniperus scopulorum* 'Tolleson's Green Weeping' (1)
2. Bird's-nest spruce, *Picea Abies* 'Nidiformis' (3)
3. Threadleaf coreopsis, *Coreopsis verticillata* 'Zagreb' (3)
4. Variegated annual vinca, *Vinca major* 'Variegata' (3)
5. French marigold, *Tagetes patula* 'Janie Flame' (7)
6. Common garden petunia, *Petunia* x *hybrida* 'White Cascade' (2)

WINDOW BOX

1. Geranium, *Pelargonium* x *hortorum* 'Orbit Scarlet' (3)
2. Common garden petunia, *Petunia* x *hybrida* 'White Cascade' (4)
3. Browallia, *Browallia speciosa* 'Blue Troll' (5)

FREESTANDING POTS AND PLANTERS

1. Climbing miniature rose, *Rosa* 'Snowfall' (1)
2. Miniature rose, *Rosa* 'Debut' (3)
3. Browallia, *Browallia speciosa* 'Silver Bells' (3)
4. Common garden petunia, *Petunia* x *hybrida* 'Ultra Crimson Star' (2)
5. Zucchini, *Cucurbita Pepo* var. *Melopepo* 'Green Magic' (1)
6. Joseph's-coat, *Amaranthus tricolor* 'Illumination' (1)
7. Sour cherry, *Prunus Cerasus* 'North Star' (1)
8. Everbearing strawberry, *Fragaria vescia* 'Tristar' (12)

9. Rose geranium, *Pelargonium graveolens* (1)
10. Swiss chard, *Beta vulgaris* 'Burpee's Rhubarb' (3)
11. Garden lettuce, *Lactuca sativa* 'Green Ice' (5)
12. Pak-choi, *Brassica Rapa* 'Mei Qing Choi' (5)
13. Cucumber, *Cucumis sativus* 'Park's Burpless Bush' (1)
14. Zinnia, *Zinnia elegans* 'Rose Pinwheel' (6)
15. Snap pea, *Pisum sativum* 'Sugar Snap' (8)
16. Rocket larkspur, *Consolida ambigua* 'Dwarf Blue Butterfly' (3)
17. Shrub rose, *Rosa* 'Bonica' (1)
18. Ageratum, *Ageratum Houstonianum* 'Adriatic' (3)
19. Common garden petunia, *Petunia* x *hybrida* 'Yellow Magic' 3)
20. Sweet alyssum, *Lobularia maritima* 'Carpet of Snow' (3)
21. Common basil, *Ocimum Basilicum* 'Spicy Globe' (1)
22. Soapweed, *Yucca glauca* (1)
23. Dill, *Anethum graveolens* 'Bouquet' (1)
24. Fennel, *Foeniculum vulgare* (1)
25. Garlic chive, *Allium tuberosum* (1)
26. Oregano, *Origanum vulgare* (1)
27. Lemon thyme, *Thymus* x *citriodorus* (1)
28. Summer savory, *Satureja hortensis* (1)
29. Spearmint, *Mentha spicata* (1)
30. Italian parsley, *Petroselinum crispum* (1)
31. Common basil, *Ocimum Basilicum* (3)
32. Creeping rosemary, *Rosmarinus officinalis* 'Prostratus' (1)
33. French lavender, *Lavandula dentata* (1)
34. Common Sage, *Salvia officinalis* (1)

A Shrub Border Garden

Joseph Hudak, a landscape architect, writes in *Taylor's Guide: Garden Design:* "Our lives are enriched through all the seasons by the bounty of trees and shrubs. They provide buffers from intense sunlight, create barriers to distracting noise and movement, mask unwanted views, modify intense winds, please the senses with their colors and scents, and bring beauty and value to any property. We could not do without them."

The garden plan depicted here fulfills these provisions by utilizing shrubs that are basically hardy, low-maintenance plants with a diversity of shapes and sizes. In addition, this border will be of interest year-round, either because of flowers, berries, or unusual bark. The trees included in this shrub border are relatively small, growing only to 25 feet (7.6 meters) or so. As such, they add height and depth to the planting without overpowering or shading too much.

The L-shaped design of this plan, shown surrounding a lawn and terrace, could be used either in the front or back of the house, screening the street or neighbors' yards. As with any border planting, the larger plants are grown at the back, with shorter plants in front. The choice of plants leads the eye around the planting.

The plants chosen for this garden were selected because of their adaptability to a wide variety of climates and soils. This planting can be done all at once or in stages. Either way, prepare the soil well by tilling an area and incorporating peat moss or other organic material into the soil. After planting, mulch with a fairly thick layer of bark chips to conserve moisture and inhibit weed growth.

Shrubs can be purchased locally at garden centers and nurseries or through mail-order catalogs. Mail-order plants are usually purchased smaller and bare-root, while those from a local source will be balled and burlapped or grown in pots. Whichever you have, be sure to dig a hole that is large enough to accommodate all of the plants' roots or soil. Plants should not be crowded or jammed into a hole that is too small. Always place the plant at the same level as it grew before. With balled-and-burlapped plants, loosen and roll back the burlap before planting; cut off the container or gently lift the plant from its tub or pot.

Adequate moisture is crucial during the first season. One of the best ways to water is by using a hose with a soaker attachment. Thoroughly soak the soil around each plant at least once a week if rainfall has been light. Beginning with the year after planting, feed shrubs each spring with a balanced fertilizer such as 5–10–10, applying at the manufacturer's recommended rate.

SCALE 1/16″ = 1′

ANNE MESKEY

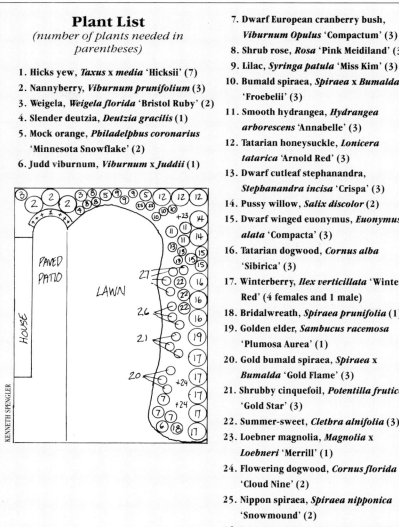

Plant List
(number of plants needed in parentheses)

1. Hicks yew, *Taxus x media* 'Hicksii' (7)
2. Nannyberry, *Viburnum prunifolium* (3)
3. Weigela, *Weigela florida* 'Bristol Ruby' (2)
4. Slender deutzia, *Deutzia gracilis* (1)
5. Mock orange, *Philadelphus coronarius* 'Minnesota Snowflake' (2)
6. Judd viburnum, *Viburnum x Juddii* (1)
7. Dwarf European cranberry bush, *Viburnum Opulus* 'Compactum' (3)
8. Shrub rose, *Rosa* 'Pink Meidiland' (3)
9. Lilac, *Syringa patula* 'Miss Kim' (3)
10. Bumald spiraea, *Spiraea x Bumalda* 'Froebelii' (3)
11. Smooth hydrangea, *Hydrangea arborescens* 'Annabelle' (3)
12. Tatarian honeysuckle, *Lonicera tatarica* 'Arnold Red' (3)
13. Dwarf cutleaf stephanandra, *Stephanandra incisa* 'Crispa' (3)
14. Pussy willow, *Salix discolor* (2)
15. Dwarf winged euonymus, *Euonymus alata* 'Compacta' (3)
16. Tatarian dogwood, *Cornus alba* 'Sibirica' (3)
17. Winterberry, *Ilex verticillata* 'Winter Red' (4 females and 1 male)
18. Bridalwreath, *Spiraea prunifolia* (1)
19. Golden elder, *Sambucus racemosa* 'Plumosa Aurea' (1)
20. Gold bumald spiraea, *Spiraea x Bumalda* 'Gold Flame' (3)
21. Shrubby cinquefoil, *Potentilla fruticosa* 'Gold Star' (3)
22. Summer-sweet, *Clethra alnifolia* (3)
23. Loebner magnolia, *Magnolia x Loebneri* 'Merrill' (1)
24. Flowering dogwood, *Cornus florida* 'Cloud Nine' (2)
25. Nippon spiraea, *Spiraea nipponica* 'Snowmound' (2)
26. Bumald spiraea, *Spiraea x Bumalda* 'Limemound' (3)
27. Dwarf red osier, *Cornus sericea* 'Kelseyi' (3)

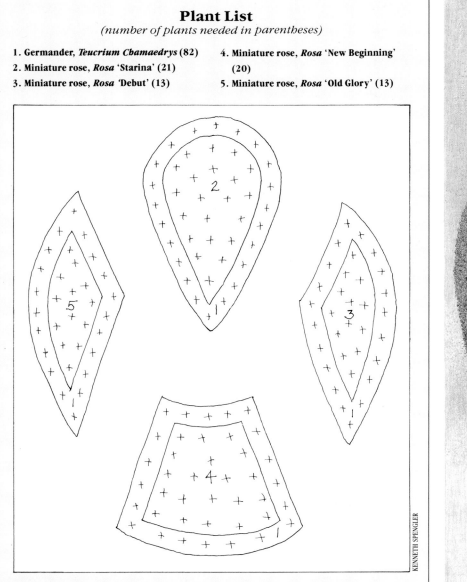

Plant List
(number of plants needed in parentheses)

1. Germander, *Teucrium Chamaedrys* (82)
2. Miniature rose, *Rosa* 'Starina' (21)
3. Miniature rose, *Rosa* 'Debut' (13)
4. Miniature rose, *Rosa* 'New Beginning' (20)
5. Miniature rose, *Rosa* 'Old Glory' (13)

KENNETH SPENGLER

SCALE 5/16″ = 1′

GRACE TVARYAN

A
Parterre
Garden

From the French phrase *broderie par terre,* or "embroidery on the ground," a parterre is a flat, open flower garden with the beds and paths arranged to form a pattern. This style of gardening reached its zenith during the reign of Louis XIV in seventeenth-century France. Enormous formal parterres of box hedges were laid out in elaborate designs. Andre LeNotre's designs in this manner for Vaux-le-Vicomte and Versailles are masterpieces of symmetry and order.

Perfectly manicured boxwood most often established the designs, while brightly colored flowers or stones added color to the interiors of each geometric shape. Although the scale at which these and similar gardens in France were created is monumental, the effect has been copied and recopied in the intervening years at a much smaller scale. Victorian gardens, both public and private, relied greatly on huge curving beds filled with bright flowers.

Both the formal annual and perennial gardens in this book draw upon this heritage in their design. The very simple parterre garden illustrated here offers a great deal of adaptability regarding site and plant substitution. For instance, this garden might be placed on a terrace, in a hidden corner of the garden, out in the middle of a perfectly manicured lawn, in an area of gravel paths, or as part of a courtyard.

Boxwood is the traditional "outline" plant for a parterre because of its fine-textured shiny dark green foliage, slow growth, and ability to withstand severe pruning. Unfortunately, it is only reliably hardy to 0 degrees F (–17 degrees C). Certain varieties, such as *Buxus microphylla* var. *koreana* 'Fiorii' can be grown further north, even with a winter mimimum of –40 degrees F (–40 degrees C).

For a beautiful dwarf hedge, germander is an excellent substitute. Hardy to –40 degrees F (–40 degrees C), this shrubby plant with shiny dark green leaves naturally grows 12 to 15 inches (30 to 38 centimeters) tall but can be clipped even lower. Germander does best in full sun, spaced 12 to 15 inches (30 to 38 centimeters) apart.

Although roses are often planted in formal beds, the use of miniature roses in this context is a departure from the more typical seasonal annual flowers used in parterres. Miniature roses are very hardy, bloom almost constantly during the growing season, and require very little care. Scaled down versions of their larger counterparts, most miniature roses grow to be 12 to 15 inches (30 to 38 centimeters) tall, although there are varieties that grow to be larger or smaller.

Miniature roses were first brought from Asia to Europe in the 1700s. Their popularity waxed and waned between then and the early 1900s, when hybridizers began doing extensive crossbreeding. Today, there are hundreds of varieties in a wide range of colors as well as flower and plant types, including climbers.

Miniature roses differ from larger roses in that they are usually grown on their own roots rather than being grafted. Plant them at the same depth as or slightly deeper than their nursery level. Roots are somewhat shallow, so an organic mulch keeps them cool and moist. Miniatures need no winter protection to 15 degrees F (–9 degrees C). If your winters go below that, surround plants in the fall with a loose, noncompacting mulch, such as oak leaves or pine boughs. Feed roses regularly throughout the growing season. Prune off dead wood in the spring; otherwise only touch-up pruning is needed.

Two of the miniature roses featured in this garden are the first minis to win the All-America Rose Selection designation: 'Debut' is a red rose with yellow at the base of the petals and 'New Beginning' is a bright orange. 'Starina' is probably the best loved of all minis; perfectly formed orange-red flowers bloom all summer above glossy, dark green leaves. 'Old Glory' has lovely deep red flowers.

GRACE TYARVANAS

A Chinese Garden

Chinese gardens distill, in symbolic form, the essence of nature. The elements of plants, rocks, and water are used to imply, not recreate, the natural landscape. Man's place in this scheme is subordinate, contemplative, and observant.

Much of the tradition of gardens in China centers on them as a place to be quiet, away from daily concerns, and either alone or in the company of very good friends. There are often small garden buildings for meditation, reflection and poetry composition. Poetry and Chinese gardens are also inextricably linked. Different parts of a garden are not only named but also given a poetic title, and several lines of poetry are written for them. Poetry competitions held along winding streams in the garden are a favorite diversion at parties.

The plants in a Chinese garden are enjoyed not only for their intrinsic beauty but also for their deeply symbolic, metaphysical significance. According to Christopher Thacker in *The History of Gardens*, old, knotted, gnarly trees embody the qualities of fortitude and grandeur, much as the enduring mountains, and as such are worthy of lengthy contemplation. Pine, mulberry, catalpa, bamboo, peach, and flowering plum are among the more significant trees in this category.

Flowers are frequently mentioned in Chinese poetry. Besides their symbolic implications, they're enjoyed for their beauty, food, flavoring, and medicinal qualities. The chrysanthemum was among the earliest of flowers to be cultivated. Native to China, yellow ones are recorded as early as the fifth century B.C.

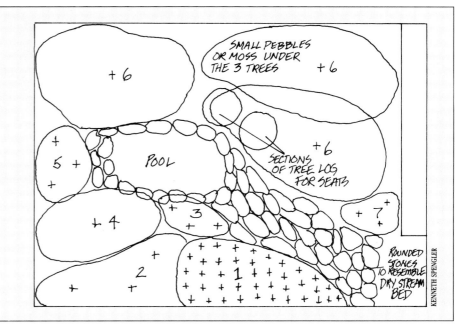

Plant List
(number of plants needed in parentheses)

1. **Blue fescue,** *Festuca ovina* var. *glauca* 'Sea Urchin' (41)
2. **Savin juniper,** *Juniperus sabina* 'Blue Forest' (3)
3. **Dwarf Norway spruce,** *Picea Abies* 'Little Gem' (3)
4. **Canadian hemlock,** *Tsuga canadensis* 'Pendula' (1)
5. **Dwarf cutleaf ninebark,** *Stephanandra incisa* 'Crispa' (3)
6. **Lace-bark pine,** *Pinus Bungeana* (3)
7. **Ostrich fern,** *Matteuccia Struthiopteris* (3)

(garden plan labels: SMALL PEBBLES OR MOSS UNDER THE 3 TREES; +6; +6; POOL; SECTIONS OF TREE LOG FOR SEATS; +6; 5 +; +4; 3; 7; 2; 1; ROUNDED STONES TO RESEMBLE DRY STREAM BED)

KENNETH SPENGLER

and are a sign of longevity. Tree peonies, hibiscus, lotus, and orchids are also significant.

Because they are the most permanent element of the natural world, rocks are essential in a Chinese landscape. Large, curiously shaped, distorted rocks are preferred. In antiquity the best stones were found in a certain lake and were deeply hollowed, riddled with holes, and curiously carved, with horizontal furrows. No matter the size or shape, large rocks must appear solidly based, with more beneath the ground than above the surface, and they must never be symmetrically arranged.

This Chinese-inspired garden plan is a cool, shady retreat for your own contemplation. Tucked into a corner of the yard between a fence and garage or storage shed, the area provides a serene oasis whether inside looking out or outside looking in.

Evergreen trees and shrubs predominate so that the garden is enjoyable year-round. Because there are few clump-forming bamboos hardy where it gets colder than –10 degrees F (–23 degrees C), I've chosen not to incorporate any into this garden; a fence of bamboo stakes will have to suffice. Where climate allows, some bamboo should definitely be included. The tufted blue fescue and blue-foliaged juniper form an unusual low-growing foreground planting. The Canadian hemlock makes a superb specimen plant and is accented with dwarf Norway spruce. Also looking as if sculpted, the mounding dwarf cutleaf stephanandra has foliage that is red in the spring and fall. The clump of ostrich fern adds an exotic touch.

This garden utilizes one of the most unusual and beautiful of all pines, the lace-bark pine.

Native to China, this round-headed tree has dark green needles and often forms a clump of several trunks. Most significant is the bark, which peels off irregularly, exposing sections of cream-colored inner bark.

The small pool can be a preformed fiberglass liner or a flexible black PVC liner. Use large, smooth stones for the path into the garden; it is meant to look like a dry stream bed. Chinese gardens do not usually have lawns, so the area under the trees could be small pebbles or moss.

To keep this a garden of serenity rather than one of maintenance and to take advantage of the shade, I suggest occasionally sinking pots of florists' mums into the ground at various spots around the garden rather than attempting to grow perennials. Finally, to make this garden uniquely yours, search out an unusual viewing stone to include in this area.

A French Garden

The grand formal gardens of seventeenth-century France, epitomized by Versailles and Chateau de Villandry, are characterized by vast flat expanses, axial paths, geometric beds, sheared trees and shrubs, walls and gates, fountains and pools, hidden woodland gardens, and statuary and urns. Elegant and refined, the classic French garden is based on symmetrical formality, geometric shapes, and an overriding sense of order. Plant material is secondary to the design, and as such, represents man prevailing over nature.

The French influence on American garden design can be readily traced to the early days of the fledgling country. Frenchman Pierre L'Enfant's 1791 plan for Washington, D.C., is directly related to the work of Andre Le Notre's at Versailles. French botanist Andre Michaux visited Charleston, South Carolina, in 1786, and the tiny, jewellike formal gardens of this city still bear testament to the French influence, incorporating many of the elements listed above.

Later, the manorial estates of the late nineteenth and early twentieth centuries such as Biltmore near Asheville, North Carolina, and Old Westbury Gardens, Old Westbury, New York, would take their inspiration from the elaborate French gardens.

The garden plan shown here is reminiscent of the French-influenced southern town-house garden. A wrought-iron fence and gate surrounds this small front yard. An especially hardy form of English ivy covers the ground along the fence and the front of the house.

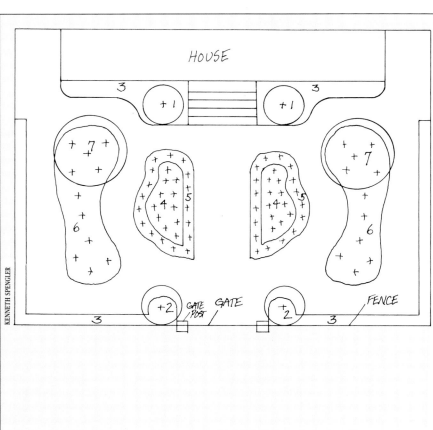

KENNETH SPENGLER

These two areas are accented by hardy hybrid blue hollies.

Two pairs of geometric beds are set into the lawn; you could also have walks of brick or gravel. The plants chosen for these areas will give a formal appearance with minimal pruning. 'Capital' callery pear naturally grows in a narrow, columnar form; masses of small white flowers are borne in spring; leaves are a glossy green and turn red in fall; and small fruits decorate the tree in winter and provide food for birds. The creeping juniper planted underneath forms a dense mat only 6 inches (15 centimeters) tall; the foliage is a silvery blue year-round.

'Crimson Pygmy' barberry is a dwarf, pur-ple-leaved plant that forms a dense, low hedge around the inkberry, which boasts shiny green leaves in summer and bright berries in winter.

This garden could also be used as a terrace or small backyard planting or adapted to a "garden room" surrounded by a tall hedge instead of the fence. It will be most effective with a house that is symmetrical in design.

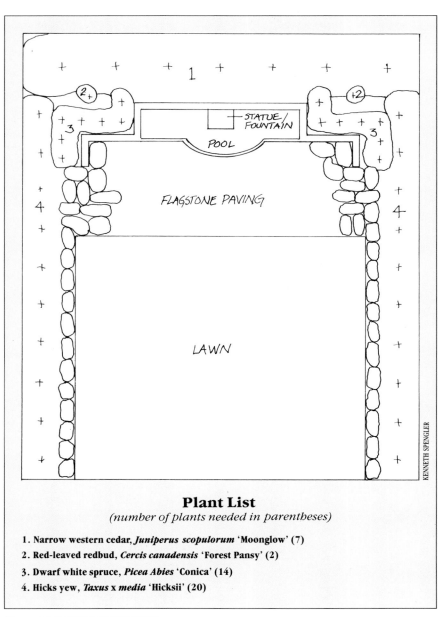

FLAGSTONE PAVING

POOL

STATUE/FOUNTAIN

LAWN

1

2

3

4

KENNETH SPENGLER

Plant List

(number of plants needed in parentheses)

1. Narrow western cedar, *Juniperus scopulorum* 'Moonglow' (7)

2. Red-leaved redbud, *Cercis canadensis* 'Forest Pansy' (2)

3. Dwarf white spruce, *Picea Abies* 'Conica' (14)

4. Hicks yew, *Taxus* x *media* 'Hicksii' (20)

GRACE TVARYANAS

An Italian Garden

The Renaissance Italian gardens have some similarity to the splendid French gardens of the seventeenth century: symmetrical, formal gardens on axes with pools, fountains, urns, statuary, and geometric beds of precisely clipped plants. There are also many differences. The most prominent distinction is that the French gardens tend to be built on flat land, while the Italian ones were many-leveled on hillsides.

The magnificent villas in the hills surrounding Rome and Florence were once summer retreats. Their owners believed that the garden was an extension of the dwelling, and as such created outdoor rooms. Immediately surrounding the villa, usually situated at the highest point, were open terraces filled with parterres of herbs and shrubs. Paths and water courses connected these to the other garden rooms lower on the hillside.

Among the various rooms would be a shaded one for dining and an outdoor theater, plus various other ones surrounded by tall hedges or stone walls. Besides the walls there was a great deal of other masonry work, including loggias, pergolas, balustrades, basins, grottoes, columns, and paving, plus the requisite statuary, urns, and finials.

Water was an essential element in every possible form: in springs, pools, fountains, cascades, falls, and sprays. It was even used in games, to activate an organ or drench the unsuspecting.

All in all, the Italian Renaissance garden was one designed for pleasure, whether it was eating, talking, watching a play, or enjoying a quiet moment of reflection.

Although the Italian-inspired garden plan shown here is only one level deep, it has many authentic aspects. To minimize maintenance, the plants surrounding the garden have naturally sculptural forms that don't require shearing. The blue-gray 'Moonglow' cedars have a narrow, columnar, pointed form reminiscent of Italian cypresses, and the dwarf white spruces repeat the shape but to a lesser height, growing slowly to 3 to 5 feet (.91 to 1.5 meters) tall. The flat-topped, columnar hicks yews form the side walls of this enclosed garden room with their dark green needles. A fence or wall on three sides of the garden would continue the theme.

Two perfectly matched 'Forest Pansy' red-leaved redbuds continue the formal symmetry. The bright pink flowers in spring are followed by deep wine red leaves. These trees grow to about 20 feet (6 meters) tall.

The centerpiece of this garden is the low stone wall and pool complete with statuary and flowing water. Flagstone or cobblestone paving in front of the pool and along the yew hedge are a natural part of this design. The lawn provides a place to relax or play. This garden could be the entire landscape on a small lot or a single room in a larger garden.

ANNE MESKEY

A Japanese Garden

A true Japanese garden is almost impossible for people of Western cultures to have since so much of one is based on inherent symbolism stemming from the tradition of nature worship that lies at the heart of the Shinto religion. Yet it is possible to have the atmosphere of serenity that is so much a part of this type of garden. Providing an area for relaxation and reflection, a Japanese-style garden can soothe and heal our hectic lives.

Through the centuries, the Japanese have taken the enjoyment of gardens and flowers to a high degree of refinement. Composing poetry while viewing the fleeting beauty of blossoms or foliage is a pastime of much pleasure and deep awareness. Joy is taken in experiencing the garden at night also.

The austere aspects of Zen Buddhism have influenced Japanese gardens since the sixteenth and seventeenth centuries, which resulted in few flowering plants to be used in landscape gardens. Flowers remain an important part of the culture, whether in a separate area close to the house or in arrangements called ikebana.

Inspired by a design from John Brookes' *The Garden Book,* this tranquil garden corner utilizes various elements often found in a Japanese garden. The boundary on two sides could be a wall or bamboo fencing. Railroad ties sunk into the ground serve as a division from the rest of the yard. The small garden area is partially paved with small round stones, and the remainder consists of a wooden deck, where one can sit and contemplate the natural scene.

In Japan, stones in a garden are selected with great care, and their symbolic position may be determined with the aid of a priest. The large stones in our little garden will not hold such significance but still should be chosen for the beauty and appeal that they may hold for us. When incorporating boulders into a garden, bury at least half of each one so that it gives the impression of belonging there.

One element of Japanese gardens that I dearly love and hope to have in my garden someday is the simple dripping bamboo pipe. Having a stone basin filled with water and a bamboo dipper gives a similar effect without having to work with pumps, electricity, and so forth.

Because cherry trees are so much a part of Japanese culture, I felt it appropriate for one to be the main plant in this garden. The white flowers of the double mazzard cherry usually last more than a week in May; the Amur cherry has single white flowers and peeling bark. Both are very hardy. As an alternative, you may want to plant a fruiting cherry, such as 'Meteor' or 'North Star.'

The colorful pink, white, and green leaves of the kolomikta vine soften the one wall; as with birds, males have the best color. Small clusters of fragrant white flowers appear in May and June. Due to the marginal hardiness of many of the best bamboos, I've chosen to use ornamental grasses instead. Eulalia's 5- to 6-foot (1.5- to 1.8-meter) leaves and flowers rustle and sway to produce a hypnotic effect. Ribbon grass is low growing with green-and-white-striped leaves. The Japanese painted fern is another graceful plant with unusual silvery-green fronds.

For me, a contemplative garden should include the beauty of flowers and the element of scent. Native to Japan, the fragrant plaintain lily offers both. During late summer and early fall, richly scented 5-inch (12-centimeter) tubular flowers arise from the glossy green leaves.

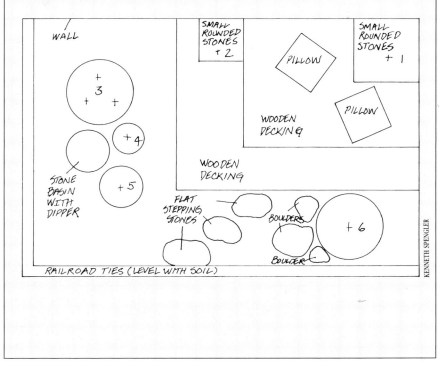

Plant List
(number of plants needed in parentheses)

1. Double mazzard cherry, *Prunus avium* 'Plena' (1), or sour cherry, *Prunus cerasus* 'North Star' or 'Meteor' (1), or Amur cherry, *Prunus Maackii* (1)
2. Kolomikta vine, *Actinidia Kolomikta* (1)
3. Eulalia, *Miscanthus sinensis* 'Gracillimus' (3)
4. Japanese painted fern, *Athyrium Goeringianum* 'Pictum' (1)
5. Fragrant plantain lily, *Hosta plantaginea* 'Grandiflora' (1)
6. Ribbon grass, *Phalaris arundinacea* var. *picta* (1)

KENNETH SPENGLER

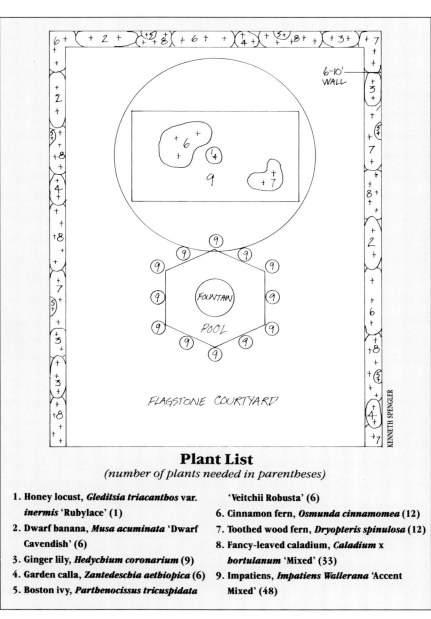

KENNETH SPENGLER

FLAGSTONE COURTYARD

6-10′ WALL

FOUNTAIN

POOL

Plant List
(number of plants needed in parentheses)

1. Honey locust, *Gleditsia triacanthos* var. *inermis* 'Rubylace' (1)
2. Dwarf banana, *Musa acuminata* 'Dwarf Cavendish' (6)
3. Ginger lily, *Hedychium coronarium* (9)
4. Garden calla, *Zantedeschia aethiopica* (6)
5. Boston ivy, *Parthenocissus tricuspidata* 'Veitchii Robusta' (6)
6. Cinnamon fern, *Osmunda cinnamomea* (12)
7. Toothed wood fern, *Dryopteris spinulosa* (12)
8. Fancy-leaved caladium, *Caladium* x *hortulanum* 'Mixed' (33)
9. Impatiens, *Impatiens Wallerana* 'Accent Mixed' (48)

A
Spanish
Garden

Much of what is considered typically Spanish, such as the gardens of the Alhambra and the Generalife, actually owe their conception to the Moors. Up until 1492, Granada had been a Moorish province for seven hundred years. Only in the same year as Columbus discovered America did Ferdinand and Isabella's armies defeat the Arabs, driving them out of the Iberian Peninsula and uniting the country.

The classic elements of the Spanish garden include an enclosed patio, low hexagonal tiled basin with a fountain, shade trees, and brightly colored and scented flowers.

The courtyard garden illustrated here incor-porates these elements but gears them for a temperate climate. The paved, walled garden has a large pool and fountain surrounded by pots of 'Accent Mixed' impatiens. This is a vari-ety that grows about 12 inches (30 centimeters) tall and is covered with 2.5-inch (6-centi-meter) flowers all season long. Put several plants in each pot to maximize the beauty and effect.

Behind the pool is a raised bed with a red-leaved honey locust; the graceful, finely tex-tured foliage contributes to the tropical feel of this garden. In spring, the tree has pendulous clusters of fragrant white flowers. The area be-neath the tree is mulched with bark chips or gravel and planted with two types of ferns, an-other tropical touch.

The walls of the garden are softened with Boston ivy. This vigorous climber spreads rap-idly and clings to walls without needing to be tied. The thick, waxy, shiny green leaves will be in three different shapes and are very toler-ant of urban pollution. After the leaves fall, the dark purple fruits provide winter interest.

Narrow beds around the sides of the garden at the base of the wall are planted with tender tropical plants. These must be dug at the end of each growing season and stored in a cool, dry place for the winter. Or you may replace them each year.

The ginger lily bears the most wonderfully fragrant 3-inch (7.6-centimeter) flowers which resemble white butterflies. Any one who has been to Hawaii should recognize them. Plants grow about 2 feet (60 centimeters) tall. The elegant white garden calla lily with its waxen blooms needs moist, humus-rich soil to grow well, just as the rest of these plants do. Fancy-leaved caladiums are unbeatable for color in a shaded garden like this. And, if you're lucky, you'll even get a banana crop!

Dappled sunlight, the tinkling sound of wa-ter, the sweet perfume of flowers, lush foliage, and dramatic colors make this Spanish patio garden a splendid, secluded retreat.

A Hillside Garden

Christopher Thacker, in *The History of Gardens* writes about the great eighteenth-century garden designer Lancelot Brown: "He was called 'Capability' Brown from his way of saying, when asked to give his opinion on a property, that the landscape or scene in question had 'capabilities' which he might be able to bring into proper prominence if allowed to undertake the task."

Brown did not try to obliterate hills, streams, and villages as was done at Versailles; rather he worked at utilizing the natural potential of a scene. The point of all this is, of course, to not despair if you have a garden that seems composed of unmanageable levels. There are a variety of solutions to a sloping site.

The most economical method is to grade the site to a gradual slope and plant with grass. A gentle gradient of 30 to 45 degrees can be safely mowed. If you want a sharply chiseled slope, plant a decorative ground cover, such as pachysandra, ivy, or vinca.

A more elaborate solution is to build retaining walls. This offers the most possibilities for landscaping. Building retaining walls is not a project to be undertaken lightly. Walls must be strong and properly constructed in order to hold the heavy pressure of soil and water. An important consideration is allowing a means for the water to drain from behind the wall.

Whether you decide to build the retaining walls yourself or have it done professionally, you will still have to decide on the type of wall you want. Walls may be constructed of even or irregular stone, brick, concrete block, poured concrete, precast concrete, railroad ties, or logs, for example. Each has their own attendant cost, longevity, and visual effect in the landscape.

Rather than one large retaining wall, this landscape utilizes three lower ones. A flight of steps adjacent to these three levels provides a rhythm and focal point to the garden, leading the eye up the hill from the garden seat to the sundial.

The plant material selected for this garden requires little care yet creates an effect often found in meticuously manicured gardens. The hedge of mentor barberry screens one side of the garden with its thick, leathery leaves, which remain evergreen in warmer climates and on the plant well into the winter in colder regions.

Both 'Skyrocket' cedar and 'Capital' callery pear have a naturally columnar appearance. The callery pear is covered with lovely white flowers in spring; these are followed by shiny leaves and small fruit that attract birds to the garden into the winter. 'Crimson Pygmy' barberry retains its low profile without trimming, and its deep maroon foliage provides subtle color to the garden.

The flower beds in front of each of the three retaining walls are planted in a very simple yet effective combination of two of my favorite annuals, 'Summer Madness' common garden petunias and 'Victoria' mealy-cup sage. These beds could be used for your favorite annuals, a mixture of annuals and perennials, or roses.

This garden provides a variety of areas for viewing and enjoying the garden, whether from below on the paved terrace or the garden seat or from above at the sundial or sheltered beneath the wisteria-covered arbor.

GRACE TVARYANAS

Plant List
(number of plants needed in parentheses)

1. Callery pear, *Pyrus calleryana* 'Capital' (2)
2. Mentor barberry, *Berberis* x *mentorensis* (14)
3. Wisteria, *Wisteria floribunda* 'Ivory Tower' (1)
4. Narrow eastern cedar, *Juniperus virginiana* 'Skyrocket' (11)
5. Japanese barberry, *Berberis Thunbergii* 'Atropurpurea Nana' or 'Crimson Pygmy' (31)
6. Mealy-cup sage, *Salvia farinacea* 'Victoria' (55)
7. Common garden petunia, *Petunia* x *hybrida* 'Summer Madness' (55)
8. Common periwinkle, *Vinca minor* (168)

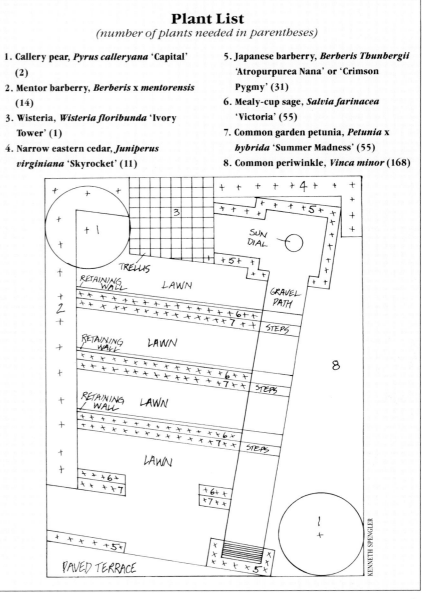

KENNETH SPENGLER

A Bird and Butterfly Garden

Anyone who thinks a garden is just plants probably hasn't been gardening for very long. A healthy garden will actually be a veritable cosmopolitan ecosystem, complete with a full range of animals, insects, and birds as well as assorted microorganisms and other critters large and small. Two of these, birds and butterflies, are among the most desired.

Even with these wonderful creatures there can be too much of a good thing sometimes, as when the birds harvest your cherries right before you want to and when caterpillars (the larval life stage of butterflies) defrock your favorite flower. But this is a small price to pay for the sound of the mockingbird's 2 a.m. trill, the cardinal's cheerful "peter, peter" in the morning, the robin's rain song, the woodpecker's persistent rat-tat-tat, the hummingbird's whirring wings, and all the other sounds in the chorus.

And, of course, the bright, flitting colors of both the birds and the butterflies add their own unique aura to the garden. Or, as naturalist Miriam Rothschild writes in *The Butterfly Gardener,* "Butterflies add another dimension to the garden for they are like dream flowers—childhood dreams—which have broken loose from their stalks and escaped into the sunshine. Air and angels."

Some people might contend that attracting birds to the garden will be to the detriment of butterflies, as the birds will feed upon the caterpillars in addition to bugs and berries. Yet unless you have some very rare butterfly species, in which case they can be sleeved or reared in cages, a balanced population of each can usually be reached.

The one thing that you will have to give up

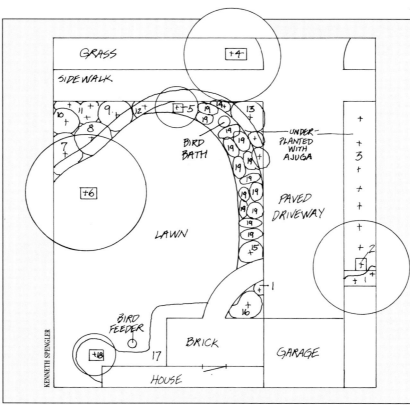

KENNETH SPENGLER

Plant List
(number of plants needed in parentheses)

1. Scarlet trumpet honeysuckle, *Lonicera x Brownii* 'Dropmore Scarlet' (3)
2. Flowering dogwood, *Cornus florida* 'Cloud Nine' (1)
3. Shrub rose, *Rosa* 'Bonica' (7)
4. Korean mountain ash, *Sorbus alnifolia* (1)
5. Allegheny serviceberry, *Amelanchier laevis* (1)
6. River birch, *Betula nigra* 'Heritage' (1)
7. Beautybush, *Kolkwitzia amabilis* (1)
8. Spicebush, *Lindera Benzoin* (1)
9. Tatarian honeysuckle, *Lonicera tatarica* 'Arnold Red' (1)
10. Bridalwreath, *Spiraea prunifolia* (1)
11. Bumald spiraea, *Spiraea x Bumalda* 'Anthony Waterer' (3)
12. Tatarian dogwood, *Cornus alba* 'Sibirica' (1)
13. Mock orange, *Philadelphus coronarius* 'Minnesota Snowflake' (1)
14. Lilac, *Syringa patula* 'Miss Kim'(3)
15. Butterfly bush, *Buddleia nanboensis* 'Petite Plum' (1)

or at least minimize in creating this sort of garden will be pesticides. At the very most you must focus on the individual pest and plant. For instance, if the cabbage and broccoli are being overrun by cabbage moth caterpillars, then spray just these with the environmentally safe *Bacillus thuringiensis;* do not spray the entire garden.

The most important aspect of encouraging birds and butterflies to your garden is to pro-

vide adequate habitat. Birds need plants that will provide food, cover, and nesting sites. Nectar plants for adult butterflies are necessary, plus larval food plants for caterpillars. Both birds and butterflies need a constant supply of fresh water.

This front-yard garden plan would be a pleasure even if the plants weren't specifically chosen for satisfying one or more of the above requirements. A 3- to 4-foot (.91- to 1.2-meter)

fence gives an enclosed feeling to this garden without totally blocking the view. Plants on both sides of it soften its lines.

There is something of interest in this garden year-round. Even in winter the beautiful bark of the birch, the unusual branches of Harry Lauder's walking stick, and the deep green leaves of the ivy will help to remind you that the world around us is to be enjoyed and lived with in harmony at all seasons. A garden of

16. Golden elder, *Sambucus racemosa* 'Plumosa Aurea' (1) underplanted with Flossflower, *Ageratum Houstonianum* 'Blue Delft; Heliotrope, *Heliotropium arborescens* 'Marine'' and Common garden petunia, *Petunia* x *hybrida* 'Summer Madness'

17. English ivy, *Hedera Helix* 'Wilsonii' (75)

18. Harry Lauder's walking stick, *Corylus Avellana* 'Contorta' (1)

19. Mixed annual and perennial flower border that includes plenty of parsley for black swallowtail caterpillars as well as such other butterfly-attractant plants as ageratum, snapdragon, aster, borage, campanula, cornflower, coreopsis, cosmos, delphinium, sweet william, heliotrope, sweet rocket, sweet alyssum, red-hot poker, stock, catnip, flowering tobacco, evening primrose, butterfly weed, geranium, petunia, phlox, mignonette, scabiosa, pale pink forms of *Sedum spectabile,* goldenrod, 'Marietta' marigolds, hyssop, nasturtium, verbena, rosemary, and lavender.

fragrance, flowers, and fruit, it will also become a haven for birds and butterflies.

The butterfly bush is reliably hardy only to −10 degrees F (−23 degrees C), so it should be treated as an annual in colder areas. Although this may seem a rather extravagant gesture, the price is inconsequential to the delight both you and the butterflies will receive with just one year's growth, especially with the smaller-growing varieties.

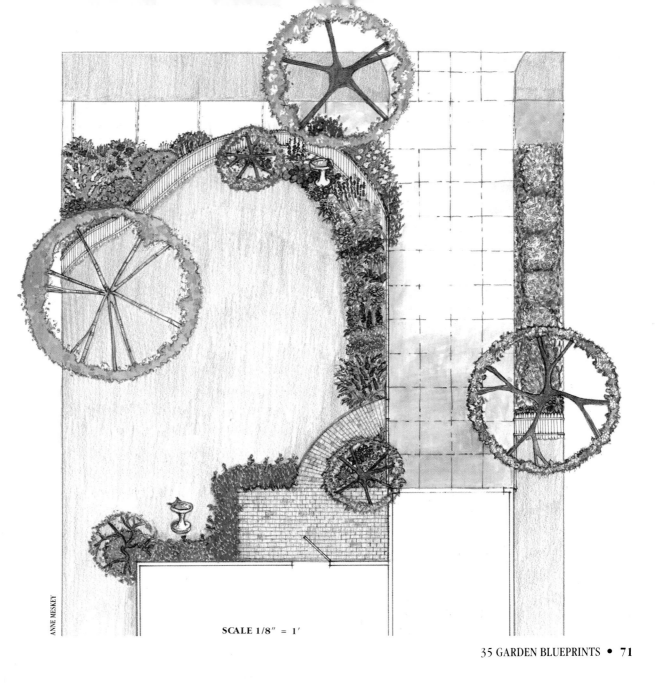

ANNE MESKEY

SCALE 1/8″ = 1′

SCALE 3/32″ = 1′

A Climbing Garden

A little whimsy, if not downright outrageousness, should be a part of everyone's life. We all need to kick up our heels a bit and play, at least occasionally. For example, this garden, composed almost entirely of climbing plants, might have been part of Alice's Wonderland. Whether or not you would ever want a yard as focused as this is on one type of plant growth, I do hope it encourages you to consider the many possibilities of "growing up."

Climbing plants are essentially any plant with long stems that are so weak that they will trail upon the ground without some external vertical support. They may be large or small and annual, perennial, or woody.

Climbing plants can serve various functions in a landscape, either enhancing or hiding features. They can also serve as ground covers. Vines climb by one of five basic methods: leaning or trailing, catching with thorns, weaving, rooting, or grasping by means of twining, clinging with tendrils, sticking with adhesive disks, or hooking.

One of the keys to success with climbing plants is having strong, well-made arbors, trellises, fences, and other supports. When building, use rot-resistant wood or wood treated with a nontoxic preservative to ensure longevity of the structures. Posts should be sunk 2 to 3 feet (60 to 91 centimeters) in the ground. If you have experience or confidence in your ability, then by all means go ahead and construct them yourself. Otherwise, hire a reliable contractor.

Many people have found a shady terrace topping of an open-grid framework makes a fine arbor for climbing plants, providing light, airy shade plus the delectable rustle of the leaves overhead. The grape at one corner not only produces wonderful fruit for eating fresh or making into jellies, jams, and juices but offers beauty throughout the seasons with lush foliage, pendant clusters of fruit, brilliant autumn color, and a network of thick, woody stems. Trumpet vine bears clusters of bright orange to scarlet trumpet-shaped flowers in midsummer.

The Boston ivy is best suited for clinging to brick or stone walls. The romantic wisteria can quickly become party to a bad affair if not given very strong support. The two other vines used along the fence, silver lace vine and Oriental bittersweet, will also need their branches tied to strong supports. If you have a chain-link fence, they can be tied directly to it; for a wood or masonry fence, use copper or galvanized wire. Although slow to become established, the climbing hydrangea will be spectacular in time.

The small arbor in the back of the garden is adorned with five different annual vines, each with beautiful, distinctive flowers. A trellis or several strings at each post will support these. Other types of annual vines are those that produce food.

Partially hidden by a large hedge of Canadian hemlock, this food-growing area utilizes pole green, lima, yard-long, and scarlet runner beans, and red-stemmed malabar spinach grown on purchased "bean towers," tomatoes in homemade concrete-reinforcing wire cages, snap peas, cucumbers, melons, and gourds

Plant List
(number of plants needed in parentheses)

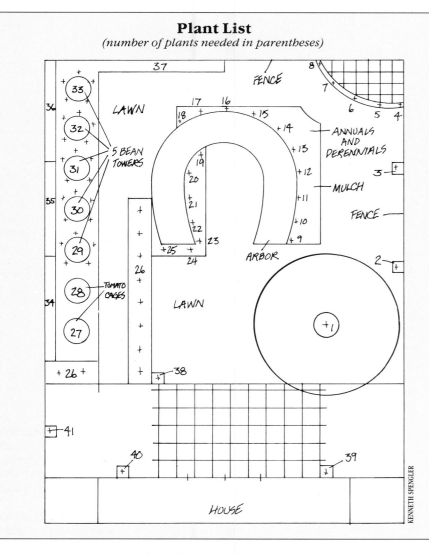

KENNETH SPENGLER

1. Climbing hydrangea, *Hydrangea anomala petiolaris* (1)
2. Oriental bittersweet, *Celastrus orbiculatus* (2)
3. Silver lace vine, *Polygonum aubertii* (1)
4. Cypress vine, *Ipomoea Quamoclit* (1)
5. Cup-and-saucer vine, *Cobaea scandens* (1)
6. Moonflower, *Ipomoea alba* (1)
7. Garden nasturtium, *Tropaoleum majus* (1)
8. Common morning-glory, *Ipomoea purpurea* 'Heavenly Blue' (1)
9. Clematis, *Clematis* 'Niobe' (1)
10. Clematis, *Clematis x jackmanii* (1)
11. Clematis, *Clematis* 'Nelly Moser' (1)
12. Clematis, *Clematis* 'Mrs. Cholmondeley' (1)
13. Clematis, *Clematis* 'Henryi' (1)
14. Clematis, *Clematis chrysocoma* var. *sericea* (1)
15. Clematis, *Clematis texensis* 'Duchess of Albany' (1)
16. Clematis, *Clematis maximowicziana* (1)
17. Clematis, *Clematis macropetala* (1)
18. Clematis, *Clematis* 'Marie Boisselot' ('Mme. LeCoultre')
19. Late Dutch honeysuckle, *Lonicera Periclymenum* 'Serotina Florida' (1)
20. Scarlet trumpet honeysuckle, *Lonicera x Brownii* 'Dropmore Scarlet' (1)
21. Everblooming honeysuckle, *Lonicera x Heckrottii* (1)
22. Climbing rose, *Rosa* 'Dortmund' (1)
23. Climbing miniature rose, *Rosa* 'Jeanne Lajoie' (1)
24. Climbing miniature rose, *Rosa* 'Snowfall' (1)
25. Climbing rose, *Rosa* 'Don Juan' (1)
26. Canadian hemlock, *Tsuga canadensis* (10)
27. Tomato, *Lycopersicon Lycopersicum* 'Sweet 100' (1)
28. Tomato, *Lycopersicon Lycopersicum* 'Better Boy' (1)
29. Malabar spinach, *Basella alba* 'Rubra' (5)
30. Lima bean, *Phaseolus lunatus* 'Carolina' (5)
31. Pole bean, *Phaseolus vulgaris* 'Kentucky Wonder' (5)
32. Scarlet runner bean, *Phaseolus coccineus* (5)
33. Yard-long bean, *Vigna unguiculata sesquipedalis* (5)
34. Sugar snap pea, *Pisum sativum* 'Sugar Snap' (1 packet)
35. Cucumber, *Cucumis sativus* 'Sweet Success' (1 packet)
36. Cantaloupe, *Cucumis Melo* 'Jenny Lind' (1 packet)
37. Mixed ornamental gourds (1 packet)
38. Grape, *Vitis Labrusca* 'Concord' (1)
39. Trumpet vine, *Campsis x Tagliabuana* 'Mme. Galen' (1)
40. Boston ivy, *Parthenocissus tricuspidata* 'Veitchii Robusta' (1)
41. Wisteria, *Wisteria floribunda* 'Ivory Tower' (1)

trained on heavy cord or netting along a fence.

It seemed fitting that the focal point of this garden, a lucky-horseshoe-shaped arbor, features what is known as the "queen of the climbers" as well as the "queen of flowers." There is also the addition of three of the best honeysuckle varieties. There are hundreds of species and hybrids of clematis, with flowers in many colors at different seasons. The ones suggested here offer a microcosm of this regal beauty.

The 'Dortmund' climbing rose is among the hardiest, while 'Don Juan' needs winter protection. 'Jeanne Lajoie' is a well-known, reliable climbing miniature rose; 'Snowfall' is newer and it shows great promise because of its exceptional vigor and hardiness.

An Herb Garden

If banished to a deserted island and given only one group of plants to take along, I would without a moment's hesitation have it be herbs. Such a choice would be far from restrictive, because the category herbs is incredibly broad. The dictionary defines them as any plant valued for its medicinal, savory, or aromatic properties, while the American Herb Society adds plants used for pleasure.

From those two perspectives it's obvious I have all manner of annuals, perennials, bulbs, shrubs, and trees at my disposal. Also obvious is that many of these plants are already in some part of the yard. In my own garden, I have intermingled them among all my other plantings. Many of the herbs work well this way and are very useful landscape elements.

Creating an area strictly for herbs is a time-honored tradition, however. Spanning centuries and continents, herb gardens were once very much a part of monasteries, medical schools, and botanical gardens. Today, when most people think of an herb garden, they envision a design based on the monastic cloister garden—divided into four segments and bisected by paths with an ornament in the center.

The garden design illustrated here is based on the planting plan of Gertrude Jekyll for the home of her collaborator, the architect Sir Edward Lutyens. The five circular, interlocking brick beds are called a *quincunx*. It is at once similar yet different from the monastic quadrant concept, with enough of each to have the feeling of tradition yet not be boring. This garden could be situated in the middle of a lawn or tucked away in its own little "garden

SCALE 5/16" = 1'

ANNE MESKEY

room'' set off and surrounded by a hedge.

In selecting the site, keep in mind that most herbs need at least six hours of sun each day. The exceptions are angelica, sweet cicely, and sweet woodruff, which need partial shade. Herbs tolerate a wide range of soil types, as long as they are well drained. Prepare the soil as you would for a flower or vegetable garden, working it up well and incorporating plenty of peat moss or compost. Fertilize lightly, as rich soil yield herbs lacking in fragrance and flavor. Mulch herb beds with shredded bark or wood chips to conserve moisture and inhibit weeds. Pests are seldom a problem.

The plants for these beds were chosen for their diversity of purpose—culinary, cosmetic, craft, dye, and historical. Many of the plants are annuals or tender perennials that will have to be replaced each year. This gives you a chance to try new ones. To keep the mints and artemisias from spreading and becoming invasive, sink flue tiles into the soil then put a plant in this space.

Gardening with herbs is a very infectious process. There is something magical about herbs that draws us into exploring and using them more and more. Avail yourself of the many excellent mail-order companies offering herbs and the wonderful books available on growing and using these fascinating plants.

Plant List

(number of plants needed in parentheses)

1. Lady's-mantle, *Alchemilla vulgaris* (3)
2. Our-lady's bedstraw, *Galium verum* (3)
3. Love-in-a-mist, *Nigella damascena* 'Persian Jewels' (8)
4. Sweet marjoram, *Origanum Majorana* (5)
5. Lamb's-ears, *Stachys byzantina* (3)
6. Woolly yarrow, *Achillea tomentosa* 'Nana' (5)
7. Fernleaf tansy, *Tanacetum vulgare* var. *crispum* (1)
8. Silver-king artemesia, *Artemisia ludoviciana* var. *albula* (1)
9. Silver horehound, *Marrubium incanum* (1)
10. Coriander, *Coriandrum sativum* (6)
11. Common basil, *Ocimum Basilicum* (3)
12. Hyssop, *Hyssopus officinalis* (1)
13. Dill, *Anethum graveolens* (3)
14. Pennyroyal, *Mentha Pulegium* (3)
15. Crete dittany, *Origanum Dictamnus* (4)
16. Curly parsley, *Petroselinum crispum* (6)
17. Garden thyme, *Thymus vulgaris* (6)
18. Catmint, *Nepeta Mussini* (3)
19. Dwarf globe amaranth, *Gomphrena globosa* 'Buddy' (8)
20. Common basil, *Ocimum Basilicum* 'Green Ruffles' (3)
21. Shisho, *Perilla frutescens* (3)
22. Chervil, *Anthriscus Cerefolium* (6)
23. Yarrow, *Achillea taygetea* 'Moonshine' (1)
24. Rosemary, *Rosmarinus officinalis* (1)
25. Common sage, *Salvia officinalis* (1)
26. Tarragon, *Artemisia Dracunculus* (1)
27. Dwarf strawflower, *Helichrysum bracteatum* 'Bright Bikinis' (8)
28. Dwarf statice, *Limonium sinuata* 'Petite Bouquet' (8)
29. Roman chamomile, *Chamaemelum nobile* (8)
30. Pot marigold, *Calendula officinalis* 'Bon Bon' (8)
31. Summer savory, *Satureja hortensis* (5)
32. Violet, *Viola odorata* 'Rosina' (6)
33. Lemon verbena, *Aloysia triphylla* (1)
34. Spearmint, *Mentha spicata* (1)
35. French sorrel, *Rumex scutatus* (1)
36. Lovage, *Levisticum officinale* (1)
37. Anise hyssop, *Agastache Foeniculum* (3)
38. Common rue, *Ruta graveolens* (1)
39. Pineapple-scented sage, *Salvia elegans* (1)
40. Lemon thyme, *Thymus* x *citriodorus* (6)
41. Chive, *Allium schoenoprasum* (6)
42. Ornamental pepper, *Capsicum annuum* 'Red Missile' (6)
43. Oregano, *Origanum vulgare* (5)
44. Signet marigold, *Tagetes tenuifolia* 'Lemon Gem' (8)
45. Pineapple mint, *Mentha suaveolens* 'Variegata' (3)
46. Lemon balm, *Melissa officinalis* (1)
47. Rose geranium, *Pelargonium graveolens* (1)
48. Common basil, *Ocimum Basilicum* 'Cinnamon' (3)
49. Southernwood, *Artemsia Abrotanum* (1)
50. Common basil, *Ocimum Basilicum* 'Citriodorum' (3)
51. Ambrosia, *Chenopodium Botrys* (3)
52. Fennel, *Foeniculum vulgare* (3)
53. Dwarf white yarrow, *Achillea Ptarmica* 'Ballerina' (8)
54. Johnny-jump-up, *Viola tricolor* (8)
55. Burnet, *Poterium Sanguisorba* (3)
56. Common basil, *Ocimum Basilicum* 'Minimum' (8)
57. Miniature rose, *Rosa* 'Sachet' (3)
58. Cowslip, *Primula veris* (8)
59. Borage, *Borago officinalis* (1)
60. Common basil, *Ocimum Basilicum* 'Dark Opal' or 'Purple Ruffles' (3)
61. Lavender cotton, *Santolina Chamaecyparissus* (1)
62. Garlic chive, *Allium tuberosum* (3)
63. English lavender, *Lavandula angustifolia* 'Hidcote' or 'Munstead' (4)
64. Italian parsley, *Petroselinum crispum* var. *neapolitanum (3)*
65. *Common wormwood, Artemisia Absinthium* 'Lambrook Silver (1)

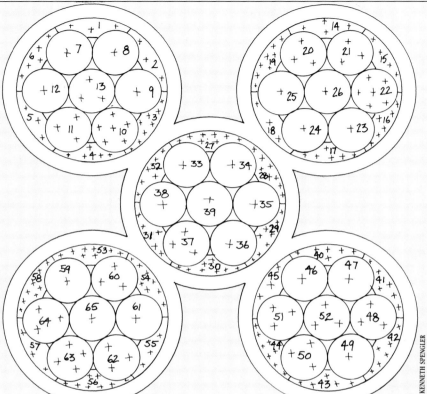

KENNETH SPENGLER

GRACE TVARYANAS

A Partial Shade Garden

In the September 1973 issue of *Flower and Garden* magazine, Helen Van Pelt Wilson wrote, ". . . shade has not precluded bloom. I have a wealth of flowers, all chosen for their shade-preference or shade-tolerance . . . please, don't consider shade a problem. It isn't. Shade is your grand opportunity for comfortable summer living, outdoors and in."

She goes on to specify that successful gardening in the shade requires four definite procedures: high and open pruning of trees, soil improvement, deep watering, and mulching.

If your property does not already have trees and you want to plant some, consider those that naturally provide high, open shade and have deep, rather than shallow, roots. These include green ash, honey locust, birch, fringe tree, dog-wood, silver bell, and sweet gum. Among these you can plant a wide variety of shrubs that tolerate or require partial shade. Some of these are forsythia, rose-of-Sharon, pieris, laurel, leucothoe, mahonia, honeysuckle, rhododendron, summer-sweet, and viburnum.

This garden plan utilizes some of the plants that Wilson championed, as well as a selection of others. There really are a surprising number of plants that do well in partial shade. (For additional ideas, see Bibliography, page 84.) This garden is shaded by a large green ash, the multistemmed river birch 'Heritage,' and three closely spaced flowering dogwoods. It is adjacent to a patio, with lawn planted to one of the newer varieties of fescue on either side. The plants suggested provide color from early spring up to frost.

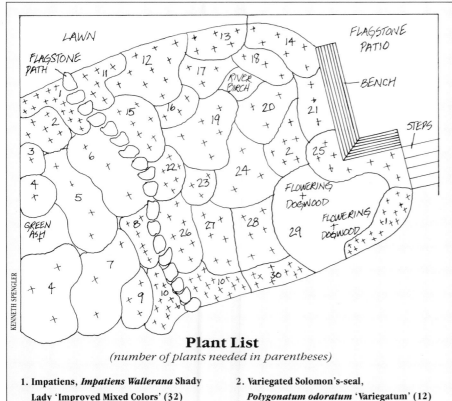

KENNETH SPENGLER

Plant List
(number of plants needed in parentheses)

1. Impatiens, *Impatiens Wallerana* Shady Lady 'Improved Mixed Colors' (32)

2. Variegated Solomon's-seal, *Polygonatum odoratum* 'Variegatum' (12)

3. Climbing hydrangea, *Hydrangea anomala petiolaris* (1)

4. Summer-sweet, *Clethra anifolia Paniculata* (4)

5. Goatsbeard, *Aruncus dioicus* 'Kneifii' (4)

6. Plantain lily, *Hosta Sieboldiana* 'Frances Williams' (6)

7. Bugbane, *Cimicifuga simplex* 'White Pearl' (3)

8. Pulmonaria, *Symphytum grandiflorum* (6)

9. Bee balm, *Monarda didyma* 'Cambridge Scarlet' (3)

10. Wax begonia, *Begonia* x *semperflorens-cultorum* 'Cocktail Mixed Colors' (25)

11. Bergenia, *Bergenia cordifolia* 'Perfect' (6)

12. Blue plantain lily, *Hosta ventricosa* (10) interplanted with Virginia bluebells, *Mertensia virginica* (6)

13. Fringed bleeding-heart, *Dicentra* 'Luxuriant' (6)

14. Lady's-mantle, *Alchemilla vulgaris* (6)

15. Astilbe, *Astilbe simplicifolia* 'Sprite' (7)

16. Bleeding-heart, *Dicentra spectabilis* (3)

17. Spiderwort, *Tradescantia* x *Andersoniana* 'Snowcap' (3)

18. Columbine, *Aqailegia* x *hybriad* 'McKana Mixed Colors' (3)

19. Astilbe, *Astilbe* x *arendsii* 'Red Sentinel' (6)

20. Grape-leaved anemone, *Anemone vitifolia* 'Robustissima' (3)

21. Toothed wood fern, *Dryopteris spinulosa* (3)

22. Lungwort, *Pulmonaria arenaria* 'Rubra' (6)

23. Lenten-rose, *Helleborus orientalis* (3)

24. Astilbe, *Astilbe tacquetii* 'Superba' (3)

25. Christmas fern, *Polystichum acrostichoides* (9)

26. Japanese painted fern, *Athyrium goeringianum* 'Pictum' (7)

27. Toad-lily, *Tricyrtis hirta* (6)

28. Astilbe, *Astilbe* x *arendsii* 'Peach Blossom' (6)

29. Sweet woodruff, *Galium odoratum* (32) interplanted with Siberian squill, *Scilla siberica* (24) and Spanish squill, *Scilla hispanica* (24)

30. Epimedium, *Epimedium grandiflorum* 'Rose Queen' (9)

A Shade Garden

I f you live in an older home, the chances are good that there is a narrow side yard with several large pine or hemlock trees, either on your property or on that of your neighbors. The shade beneath these trees is very dense, allowing few plants to grow there. Even so, you can have a lush hideaway of a garden in such a spot.

First, if possible, trim the lower limbs from the trees so you can move around and so some light will filter through the limbs. Next, plan on working the soil up well, incorporating plenty of organic matter before planting. Once planted, you will have to fertilize at least every spring. Most important to success, especially with the plants in this plan, is to water them regularly—a thorough soaking once a week is best. Mulch around the plants to help the plants hold moisture. Once established, this garden will be very low maintenance.

The 'Frances Williams' plantain-lily has been voted the favorite hosta of the American Hosta Society. It is large, bold, dramatic, tropical looking, and expensive. Yet what a spectacular accent it is!

Caladiums are tender bulbs that will have to be dug up in the fall and stored over winter in a cool basement. The fuchsias or begonias are not hardy either, yet they can also be kept indoors from year to year. Or, just buy new ones each spring.

The ferns chosen contribute to the exotic feel of this garden. If kept well watered, some of them will reach 4 to 6 feet (1.2 to 1.8 meters) tall. The Christmas fern planted around the bench is much smaller.

Two elements especially add to the special quality of this garden. One is the small stone water basin. This might be purchased at a garden center, or it could be a special rock found on an exploration along a riverbank. Japanese gardens, such as the one in Portland, Oregon, or Brooklyn, New York, incorporate a bamboo pipe that slowly drips into the stone bowl. The second item that sets this garden apart is the addition of a piece of sculpture. I have a large, bold blue monolith in my garden, but your taste may tend toward another style.

Plant List
(number of plants needed in parentheses)

1. Fuchsia, *Fuchsia* x *hybrida* or Skaugum begonia, *Begonia worthiana* (3) in pots on pedestals
2. Fancy-leaved caladium, *Caladium* x *hortulanum* (18)
3. Christmas fern, *Polystichum acrostichoides* (28)
4. Plantain lily, *Hosta* 'Shade Fanfare' (3)
5. Royal fern, *Osmunda regalis* (15)
6. Lady fern, *Athyrium filix-femina* (6)
7. Cinnamon fern, *Osmunda cinnamomea* (6)
8. Ostrich fern, *Matteuccia Struthiopteris* (12)
9. Plantain lily, *Hosta* 'Frances Williams' (3)

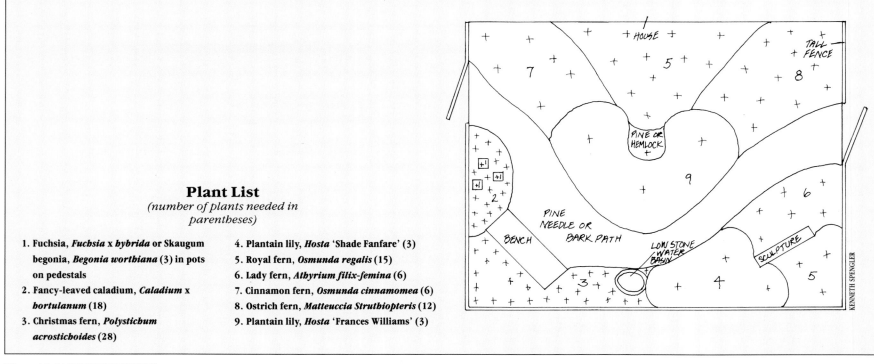

GRACE TVARYANAS

GRACE TVARVANAS

A Terrace Garden

Inspired by a photo of an inviting garden in a magazine advertisement, this garden satisfies two definitions of the word "terrace." Directly adjacent to the house is a paved area, or terrace, running the full width of the lot. Behind that, an irregular series of vertical embankments, or walls, create a terrace on the steep lot so that the area beyond is relatively flat.

The paved terrace, or patio, literally increases the size of your home by providing additional space for working, eating, playing, and entertaining. It also serves as a transition between the house and garden with its tubs and pots of flowers (or, as the container garden plan in this book illustrates, with a full range of plants, including trees, shrubs, herbs, fruits, and vegetables as well as flowers.)

What you choose as the paving material depends on cost, use, and what is most readily available in your area. For a heavily used site, a solid paving material is most desirable. A poured-concrete slab is durable and inexpensive but tends to look a bit utilitarian. Bricks give a warm, comfortable appearance; because they are small and uniform, they tend to enlarge a space. Larger pavers, such as flagstone or manufactured aggregate stone, also make an area seem smaller. Either brick or pavers can be mortared to a concrete slab or placed on top of soil or sand.

Railroad ties laid horizontally and upright timbers in uneven lengths are the materials used in the retaining walls. These should either be pressure treated or pretreated with copper

Plant List
(number of plants needed in parentheses)

1. Honey locust, *Gleditsia triacanthos* var. *inermis* 'Sunburst' (1)
2. Chinese juniper, *Juniperus chinensis* 'Gold Coast' (3)
3. Spreading juniper, *Juniperus horizontalis* 'Emerald Spreader' (13)
4. Dwarf mugho pine, *Pinus Mugo* var. *Mugo* (3)
5. Bird's-nest spruce, *Picea Abies* 'Nidiformis' (5)
6. Japanese spurge, *Pachysandra terminalis* (46)
7. River birch, *Betula nigra* 'Heritage' with multiple stems (1)
8. Lavelle hawthorn, *Crataegus* x *Lavallii* (1)
9. Common periwinkle, *Vinca minor* (285)
10. Korean mountain ash, *Sorbus alnifolia* (1)
11. Pots and tubs of annuals

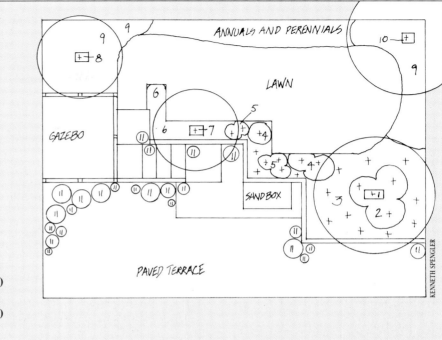

KENNETH SPENGLER

napthanate to retard decay, or you can choose a wood that is decay resistant but more expensive. Because a retaining wall must be able to withstand such immense pressure, I strongly urge you to either read several good books on the subject if you want to do it yourself or have the job done by a reliable contractor.

A series of steps and landings as well as a gazebo provide a transition between the two levels. These, also, should be constructed of either treated lumber or decay-resistant wood. The gazebo provides a sheltered, shaded spot for dining or entertaining as well as a place for hanging baskets of flowers. If you don't have children, use the area designated for a sandbox as a planter.

The area behind the wall, steps, and gazebo contains a small, perfectly manicured lawn; a long, narrow flower border; and several shade trees underplanted with low-maintenance ground covers and evergreens.

The honey locust has a delicate, elegant look that belies its adaptability; new leaves are a bright golden color that contrasts with the dark green, older foliage. At the base of this tree are three low, spreading junipers with graceful, lacy golden foliage.

The 'Heritage' river birch is an excellent substitute for the white-barked birches because it is resistant to the bronze birch borer, is tolerant of temperature extremes, and has lovely pinkish-white to tan peeling bark. I suggest searching out a clump form rather than one with a single trunk. The Japanese spurge

ground cover has bright, glossy evergreen leaves. Both the dwarf mugho pine and bird's-nest spruce are slow-growing, compact, roundish conifers.

The lavelle hawthorn is a small tree with upright branches and dark green leaves. Large white flowers appear among these during late spring and early summer, followed by vivid orange fruit that stays on the tree through much of the winter. Korean mountain ash also has white flowers that develop into orange-red fruit. Fall leaf color is yellow to orange. Common periwinkle is an old-fashioned ground cover that's hard to beat. Small, dark evergreen leaves cover the thin branches; its azure blue flowers provide one more reason to look forward to spring.

Bibliography

Liberty Hyde Bailey Hortorium. *Hortus Third.* New York: Macmillan. 1976.

Ball, Jeff. *Jeff Ball's 60-Minute Garden.* Emmaus, Penn.: Rodale Press. 1985.

Barton, Barbara J. *Gardening By Mail 2.* Tusker Press. 1987.

Beckstrom, Robert J. *Deck Plans.* Chevron Chemical Co. 1985.

Beley, Jim. *Garden Construction.* Chevron Chemical Co. 1985.

Brookes, John. *The Garden Book.* New York: Crown. 1984.

———. *The Small Garden Book.* New York: Van Nostrand Reinhold. 1978.

Burke, Ken, project ed. *All About Roses.* Chevron Chemical Co. 1983.

Chamberlin, S., and J. Pollock. *Fences, Gates & Walls: How to Design and Build.* HP Books. 1983.

Coats, Peter. *The House & Garden Book of Beautiful Gardens Round the World.* Little Brown & Co. 1985.

Cooper, Guy, and Gordon Taylor. *English Herb Gardens.* Rizzoli. 1986.

Cravens, Richard H. *The Time-Life Encyclopedia of Gardening: Vines.* Time-Life Books. 1979.

Creasy, Rosalind. *The Complete Book of Edible Landscaping.* Sierra Club Books. 1982.

DeWolf, Gordon P., Jr. *Taylor's Guides.* Houghton Mifflin. 1986, 1987, and 1988.

Douglas, William Lake. *Hillside Gardening.* New York: Simon & Schuster. 1987.

Edinger, Phillip, ed. *Roses.* Menlo Park, Calif.: Lane Publishing Co. 1980.

Fell, Derek. *Annuals: How to Select, Grow and Enjoy.* HP Books. 1983.

———. *Vegetables: How to Select, Grow and Enjoy.* HP Books. 1982.

Fogle, David P., Catherine Mahan, and Christopher Weeks. *Clues to American Gardens.* Starhill Press. 1987.

Foster, Gertrude B., and Rosemary F. Louden. *Park's Success With Herbs.* Geo. W. Park Seed Co. 1980.

Foster, H. Lincoln and Laura Louise Foster. *Rock Gardening: A Guide to Growing Alpines and Other Wildflowers in the American Garden.* Portland, Ore.: Timber Press. 1982.

Frederick, William H., Jr. *100 Great Garden Plants.* Portland, Ore.: Timber Press. 1986.

Graf, Alfred Byrd. *Tropica* 3rd ed. Roehrs Co. 1986.

Harper, Pamela, and Frederick McGourty. *Perennials: How to Select, Grow and Enjoy.* HP Books. 1985.

Harpur, Jerry. *The Gardener's Garden.* Boston: David R. Godine. 1985.

Hebb, Robert S. *Low Maintenance Perennials.* Quadrangle/The New York Times Book Co. 1975.

Hendrikson, Robert. *The Berry Book.* New York: Doubleday & Co. 1981.

Hill, Lewis. *Fruits and Berries for the Home Garden.* NewYork: Alfred A. Knopf. 1977.

Hobhouse, Penelope. *A Book of Gardening.* Little, Brown and Co. 1986.

Lathrop, Norma Jean. *Herbs: How to Select, Grow and Enjoy.* HP Books. 1981.

Kowalchik, Claire, and William H. Hylton, eds. *Rodale's Illustrated Encyclopedia of Herbs.* Emmaus, Penn.: Rodale Press. 1987.

Landis, Michael, and Ray Moholt. *Patios & Decks: How to Plan, Build & Enjoy.* HP Books. 1983.

Lees, Carlton B. *New Budget Landscaping.* Holt, Rinehart and Winston. 1979.

MacCaskey, Michael. *Lawns and Ground Covers: How to Select, Grow and Enjoy.* HP Books. 1982.

Nelson, William R., Jr. *Landscaping Your Home.* Univ. of Illinois College of Agriculture Cooperative Extension Service Circular 858. 1963.

New England Wild Flower Society. *Nursery Sources: Native Plants and Wildflowers.* New England Wildflower Society. 1988.

Ortho Books. *Do-It-Yourself Garden Construction Know-How.* Chevron Chemical Co. 1975.

Oster, Maggie. *Gifts and Crafts From the Garden.* Emmaus, Penn.: Rodale Press. 1988.

Ottesen, Carole. *The New American Garden.* Macmillan. 1988.

Paterson, Allen. *Plants for Shade and Woodland.* Fitzhenry & Whiteside. 1987.

Perl, Phillip. *The Time-Life Encyclopedia of Gardening: Cacti and Succulents.* Time-Life Books. 1978.

Proulx, E. Annie. *Plan and Make Your Own Fences & Gates, Walkways, Walls, & Drives.* Emmaus, Penn.: Rodale Press. 1983.

Ray, Richard, and Michael MacCaskey. *Roses: How to Select, Grow and Enjoy.* HP Books. 1981.

Rense, Paige, ed. *Gardens: Architectural Digest.* Los Angeles: The Knapp Press. 1983.

Rothschild, Miriam, and Clive Farrell. *The Butterfly Gardener.* Michael Joseph Ltd./The Rainbird Publishing Group. 1983.

Sabuco, John J. *The Best of the Hardiest.* 2nd ed. Good Earth Publishing. 1987.

Schenk, George. *The Complete Shade Gardener.* Houghton Mifflin. 1984.

Schinz, Marina, and Susan Littlefield. *Visions of Paradise.* New York: Stewart, Tabori & Chang. 1985.

Strombeck, Janet A., and Richard H. *Backyard Structures, Designs & Plans.* Sun Designs, Rexstrom Co.

———. *Gazebos and Other Garden Structures.* Sun Designs, Rexstrom Co. 1983.

Strong, Roy. *A Small Garden Designer's Handbook.* Conran Octopus. 1987.

Strong, Roy. *Creating Small Gardens.* Conran Octopus. 1986.

Swanson, Faith H, and Virginia B. Rady. *Herb Garden Design.* Univ. Press of New England. 1984.

Thacker, Christopher. *The History of Gardens.* Univ. of California Press. 1979.

Thomas, Charles B. *Water Gardens for Plants and Fish.* TFH Publications. 1988.

Toogood, Alan. *Roses in Gardens.* Salem House. 1987.

Warde, John, ed. *The Backyard Builder.* Emmaus, Penn.: Rodale Press. 1985.

Warren, E. J. M. *The Country Diary Book of Creating A Butterfly Garden.* Michael Joseph Ltd./Webb & Bower. 1988.

Williams, Robin. *Planning A Small Garden.* William Collins Sons & Co. 1988.

Wilson, Helen Van Pelt. *Successful Gardening With Perennials.* New York: Doubleday & Co. 1976.

Wyman, Donald. *Wyman's Gardening Encyclopedia.* New York: Macmillan. 1977.

Sources

In the best of all possible worlds, we would all live just down the road from a nursery or garden center with an extensive inventory of the finest plant varieties. These plants, of course, would also be perfectly suited for the particular climate and soil of the area. Ten years ago this seemed a wild, impossible dream, but today as consumers are becoming more knowledgeable and demanding, wholesalers and retailers are responding with a wider selection of plants.

Even so, there will always be a niche for the mail-order supplier, whether it be the specialist who carries the very latest or most unusual plants or the generalist who supplies those who don't have a good nursery nearby or who just prefer to shop by mail.

Abbey Gardens
4620 Carpinteria Avenue
Carpinteria, California 90313
Cacti and succulents; Catalog available

Alternative Garden Supply
3439 E. 86th Street, Suite 259
Indianapolis, Indiana 46240
Supplies and tools; Catalog available

American Sundials
Box 677, 300 Main Street
Pt. Arena, California 95468
Bronze sundials; Catalog available

Antique Rose Emporium
Route 5, Box 143
Brenham, Texas 77833
Old garden roses and perennials; Catalog available

ANZA Architectural Wood Products
Box 453
Fairfax, California 94390
Modular planters and benches

Appalachian Gardens
P.O. Box 82
Waynesboro, Pennsylvania 17268
Ornamental trees and shrubs

Appalachian Wildflower Nursery
Route 1, Box 275A
Honey Creek Road
Reedsville, Pennsylvania 17084
Rock garden plants and perennials; Catalog available

Ascot Designs
286 Congress Street
Boston, Massachusetts 02210
Ornaments and paving

Autumn Forge
1104 N. Buena Vista Avenue
Orlando, Florida 32818
Custom-made ironwork; Catalog available

Autumn Innovations
Box 28426
Greensboro, North Carolina 27419
Garden ornaments

The Banana Tree
715 Northampton Street
Easton, Pennsylvania 18042
Bananas and tropical plants; Catalog available

Bee Rock Herb Farm
5807 Sawyer Road
Signal Mountain, Tennessee 37377
Herbs, perennials, books, and supplies; Catalog available

Beersheba Wildflower Garden
Box 551, Stone Door Road
Beersheba Springs, Tennessee 37305
Southeastern wildflowers

Dorothy Biddle Service
U.S. Route 6
Greeley, Pennsylvania 18425
Flower arranging supplies and books; Catalog available

Bird 'n Hand
40 Pearl Street
Framingham, Massachusetts 01701
Bird feeding supplies

Bisnaga Cactus Nursery
Box 787-108
1132 East River Road
Belen, New Mexico 87002
Hardy cacti; Catalog available

Kurt Bluemel
2740 Greene Lane
Baldwin, Maryland 21013
Ornamental grasses, perennials, bamboos, ferns, and aquatics; Catalog available

Bluestone Perennials
7211 Middle Ridge Road
Madison, Ohio 44057
Perennials

Boehlke's Woodland Gardens
W 140 N 10829 Country Aire Road
Germantown, Wisconsin 53022
Native plants and hardy perennials; Catalog available

Bonide Chemical Company
2 Wurz Avenue
Yorkville, New York 13495
Organic and inorganic pesticides; Catalog available

Brighton By-Products
Box 23
New Brighton, Pennsylvania 15066
Landscaping supplies; Catalog available

Brittingham Plant Farms
Box 2538
Salisbury, Maryland 21801
Small fruits and asparagus

W. Atlee Burpee & Company
300 Park Avenue
Warminster, Pennsylvania 18974
Seeds and plants; annuals, perennials, bulbs, herbs, everlastings, trees, shrubs, fruit, supplies, and books

Busse Gardens
Route 2, Box 238
Cokato, Minnesota 55321
Perennials; Catalog available

C & C Products
Route 3, Box 438
Hereford, Texas 79045
Supplies

The Cactus Patch
Box 71
Radium, Kansas 67571
Hardy cacti; Catalog available

Caladium World
Drawer 629
Sebring, Florida 33871
Caladium bulbs

Camelot North
Route 2, Box 398
Pequot Lakes, Minnesota 56472
*Everlastings, perennials, and
herbs; Catalog available*

Canyon Creek Gardens
3527 Dry Creek Road
Oroville, California 95965
Perennials; Catalog available

Carroll Gardens
Box 310, 444 E. Main Street
Westminster, Maryland 21157
*Perennials, herbs, roses, vines, bulbs,
trees, and shrubs; Catalog available*

Carruth Studio
7035 N. River Road
Waterville, Ohio 43566
Hand-carved ornaments; Catalog available

The Clapper Company
1121 Washington Street
West Newton, Massachusetts 02165
Tools, supplies, books, and furniture

Clifford's Perennial & Vine
Route 2, Box 320
East Troy, Wisconsin 53120
*Perennials, clematis, and vines; Catalog
available*

Coastal Gardens & Nursery
Route 3, Box 40
4611 Socastee Boulevard
Myrtle Beach, South Carolina 29577
*Perennials, ornamental grasses, ground
covers, shrubs, and aquatics*

J Collard
Box 40098
Long Beach, California 90804
Tools and supplies

Companion Plants
7247 N. Coolville Ridge Road
Athens, Ohio 45701
Herb plants and seeds; Catalog available

Comstock, Ferre & Company
263 Main Street, Box 125
Wethersfield, Connecticut 06109
*Annual, perennial, vegetable,
and everlastings seed*

Conley's Garden Center
Boothbay Harbor, Maine 04538
Native plants; Catalog available

The Cook's Garden
Box 65, Moffits Bridge
Londonderry, Vermont 05148
*Specialty vegetable and
edible flower seeds; Catalog available*

Country Casual
17317 Germantown Road
Germantown, Maryland 20874
Wooden garden furniture; Catalog available

The Country Garden
Route 2, Box 455A
Crivitz, Wisconsin 54114
*Annual, perennial, and
everlastings seed and
perennial plants*

Country House Floral Supply
Box 86, BVL Station
Andover, Massachusetts 01810
Flower arranging supplies

Cricket Hill Herb Farm Ltd.
Glen Street
Rowley, Massachusetts 01969
*Herb plants, seeds, and books; Catalog
available*

Crownsville Nursery
Box 797, 1241 Generals Highway
Crownsville, Maryland 21032
*Perennials, ornamental grasses, herbs,
wildflowers, and ferns; Catalog available*

Dabney Herbs
Box 22061
Louisville, Kentucky 40222
*Herbs, perennials, wildflowers, books,
and supplies; Catalog available*

The Daffodil Mart
Route 3, Box 794
Gloucester, Virginia 23061
Bulbs, supplies, and books

Dalen Products
11110 Gilbert Drive
Knoxville, Tennessee 37932
Supplies; Catalog available

John Deere Catalog
1400 Third Avenue
Moline, Illinois 61265
*Tools, supplies, books,
and ornaments*

Peter De Jager Bulb Company
Box 2010, 188 Asbury Street
South Hamilton, Massachusetts 01982
Hardy bulbs

DeGiorgio Company
Box 413, 1409 3rd Street
Council Bluffs, Iowa 51502
*Annual, perennial, and vegetable
seeds; Catalog available*

Desert Nursery
1301 S. Copper
Deming, New Mexico 88030
Hardy cacti; Catalog available

Dionysos' Barn
Box 31
Bodines, Pennsylvania 17722
*Herb plants;
Catalog available*

Down to Earth Distributors
850 W. 2nd Street
Eugene, Oregon 97402
Organic supplies and tools

The Dramm Company
Box 528
Manitowic, Wisconsin 54220
*Watering equipment, tools,
and supplies*

Duncraft
33 Fisherville Road
Penacook, New Hampshire 03303
Bird feeding supplies

Dutch Gardens
P.O. Box 200
Adelphia, New Jersey 07710
Hardy and tender bulbs

Dutch Mountain Nursery
7984 N. 48th Street
Augusta, Michigan 49012
*Ornamental fruiting plants to attract
wildlife; Catalog available*

Earthstar Herb Gardens
438 W. Perkinsville Road
Chino Valley, Arizona 86323
*Herb plants and seeds;
Catalog available*

Edible Landscaping
Box 77
Afton, Virginia 22920
Unusual fruit

Erkins Studio
604 Thames Street
Newport, Rhode Island 02840
*Garden furniture, fountains, and ornaments;
Catalog available*

Henry Field Seed & Nursery Company
407 Sycamore
Shenandoah, Iowa 51602
*Vegetable and flower seeds, fruits,
trees, shrubs, roses, and supplies*

Flora Favours
Route 4, Box 370
Elkhorn, Wisconsin 53121
Perennials; Catalog available

Florentine Craftsmen
46-24 28th Street
Long Island City, New York 11101
*Garden furniture, fountains, ornaments;
Catalog available*

Florist Products
2242 North Palmer Drive
Schaumburg, Illinois 60173
Tools and supplies

Flowerland
Box 26
Wynot, Nebraska 68792
*Perennials;
Catalog available*

Dean Foster Nurseries
Box 127, 511 S. Center Street
Hartford, Michigan 49067
Fruit and nut plants

Fox Hill Farm
Box 9, 440 W. Michigan Avenue
Parma, Michigan 49269
Herbs

Full Circle Garden Products
Box 6
Redway, California 95560
Tools and supplies; Catalog available

The Garden Concepts Collection
4646 Poplar Avenue
Memphis, Tennessee 38117
Furnishings; Catalog available

Gardener's Eden
Box 7307
San Francisco, California 94120
Tools and supplies

Gardener's Supply Company
128 Intervale Road
Burlington, Vermont 05401
Tools and supplies

Garden Perennials
Route 1
Wayne, Nebraska 68787
Perennials; Catalog available

Garden Place
Box 388, 6870 Heisley Road
Mentor, Ohio 44061
Perennials; Catalog available

Garden World
2503 Garfield Street
Laredo, Texas 78043
Bananas and others; Catalog available

Gardens of the Blue Ridge
Box 10, U.S. 221 North
Pineola, North Carolina 28662
Native plants; Catalog available

Louis Gerardi Nursery
Route 1, Box 428
Geneva, Ohio 44041
Trees and shrubs

Girard Nurseries
Box 428, 6801 North Ridge
Geneva, Ohio 44041
Trees, shrubs, fruits, and ornamental grasses

Gladside Gardens
61 Main Street
Northfield, Massachusetts 01360
*Tender bulbs and perennials; Catalog
available*

Gloria Dei
36 East Road
High Falls Park
High Falls, New York 12440
Miniature roses

Golden Bough Tree Farm
Marlbank, Ontario
Canada K0K 2L0
Fruit trees and grapes; Catalog available

Goodwin Creek Gardens
Box 83
Williams, Oregon 97544
*Everlastings, herb, and wildflower seeds;
Catalog available*

Russell Graham, Purveyor of Plants
4030 Eagle Crest Road N. W.
Salem, Oregon 97304
*Unusual bulbs, ferns, trillium, and
ornamental grasses; Catalog available*

Great Lakes IPM
10220 Church Road N. E.
Vestaburg, Michigan 48891
*Supplies for integrated pest
management*

Green Earth Organics
9422 144th Street East
Puyallup, Washington 98373
Organic supplies

The Greener Thumb
Box 704
Littlefield, Texas 79339
Supplies and tools

Griffey's Nursery
1680 Highway 25-70
Marshall, North Carolina 28753
Southeastern native plants

Gurney Seed & Nursery Company
2nd & Capital
Yankton, South Dakota 57078
Vegetable and flower seeds, shrubs, and roses

Harmony Farm Supply
Box 451, 4050 Ross Road
Graton, California 95444
Fruits and supplies; Catalog available

Harris Seeds
3670 Buffalo Road
Rochester, New York 14624
Flower and vegetable seeds and supplies

Hartman's Herb Farm
Old Dana Road
Barre, Massachusetts 01005
Herb plants and supplies; Catalog available

Hartmann's Plantation
Box E, 310 60th Street
Grand Junction, Michigan 49056
Blueberries and unusual fruit

Hastings
Box 4274
Atlanta, Georgia 30302
Flower seed and fruit for the south

Phillip Hawk & Company
159 E. College Avenue
Pleasant Gap, Pennsylvania 16823
Stone lanterns; Catalog available

The Herbfarm
32804 Issaquah-Fall City Road
Fall City, Washington 98024
Herb plants and supplies

Heritage Sundial
7340 E. 131st Street
Bixby, Oklahoma 74008
Sundials

Hermitage Gardens
Box 361
Canastota, New York 13032
Water garden supplies

Hidden Spring Nursery
Route 14, Box 159
Cookeville, Tennessee 38501
Herbs and fruits; Catalog available

High Country Rosarium
1717 Downing Street
Denver, Colorado 80218
Roses; Catalog available

Holbrook Farm & Nursery
Route 2, Box 2238
Fletcher, North Carolina 28732
Perennials, and trees; Catalog available

Hyde Bird Feeder Company
Box 168
Waltham, Massachusetts 02254
Bird feeding supplies

I.F.M.
333B Ohme Garden Road
Wenatchee, Washington 98801
Organic supplies

Idaho Wood Industries
Box 488
Sandpoint, Idaho 83864
Wood garden lights

Intermountain Cactus
2344 South Redwood Road
Salt Lake City, Utah 84119
Hardy cacti; Catalog available

Inter-State Nurseries
Box 208
Hamburg, Iowa 51640
Perennials, bulbs, trees, shrubs, and fruit

Jackson & Perkins Company
Box 1028
Medford, Oregon 97501
Roses

Johnny's Selected Seeds
Box 2580
Albion, Maine 04910
Vegetable and annual seeds and supplies

J. W. Jung Seed Company
335 S. High Street
Randolph, Wisconsin 53957
Flower and vegetable seeds, and perennials

Justice Miniature Roses
5947 S. W. Kahle Road
Wilsonville, Oregon 97070
Miniature roses

David Kay Garden & Gift Catalogue
4509 Taylor Lane
Cleveland, Ohio 44128
Tools, supplies, and gifts

Kelly Nurseries of Dansville
19 Maple Street
Dansville, New York 14437
Trees, shrubs, and fruit

The Keth Company
Box 645
Corona del Mar, California 92625
Flower arranging supplies; Catalog available

Sue Fisher King
3075 Sacramento Street
San Francisco, California 18950
Planters, seats, and gazebos; Catalog available

Kinsman Company
River Road
Point Pleasant, Pennsylvania 18950
Tools, equipment, and arbors

Klehm Nursery
Route 5, Box 197
South Barrington, Illinois 60010
Perennials, specializing in peonies, daylilies, and hostas; Catalog available

Krider Nurseries
Box 29
Middlebury, Indiana 46540
Fruits, roses, trees, and shrubs

Lamb Nurseries
E. 101 Sharp Avenue
Spokane, Washington 99202
Perennials, vines, ground covers, clematis, shrubs, and rock garden plants

Lawyer Nursery
950 Highway 200 West
Plains, Montana 59859
Shrubs, trees, fruits

C. M. Leonard
Box 816
Piqua, Ohio 45356
Tools, supplies, and equipment

W. O. Lessard Nursery
19201 S. W. 248th Street
Homestead, Florida 33031
Bananas; Catalog available

Lexigrow
Box 1491
Indianapolis, Indiana 46206
Fabric mulch

Liberty Seed Company
Box 806
New Philadelphia, Ohio 44663
Vegetable and flower seeds and supplies

Lilypons Water Gardens
Box 10, 6885 Lilypons Road
Lilypons, Maryland 21717
Water lilies and aquatics; Catalog available

Little Valley Farm
Route 1, Box 287
Richland Center, Wisconsin 53581
Midwestern native plants; Catalog available

Long Hungry Creek Nursery
Red Boiling Springs, Tennessee 37150
Unusual apples

Lost Prairie Herb Farm
805 Kienas Road
Kalispell, Montana 59901
Herbs and perennials; Catalog available

Kenneth Lynch & Sons
78 Danbury Road
Wilton, Connecticut 06897
Garden furniture; Catalog available

McClure & Zimmerman
1422 W. Thorndale
Chicago, Illinois 60660
Hardy and tender bulbs

McDermott Garden Products
Box 129
1300 S. Grand Avenue
Charles City, Iowa 50616
Planters and composter

Mrs. McGregor's Garden Shop
4801 First Street N.
Arlington, Virginia 22203
*Planters, tools, gifts, and
ornaments*

Makielski Berry Farm & Nursery
7130 Platt Road
Ypsilanti, Michigan 48197
*Strawberries, cane berries,
currants, rhubarb, asparagus,
grapes, and PJM rhododendron*

Marion Designs
594 Front Street
Marion, Massachusetts 02738
Redwood furniture; Catalog available

Marvin's Cactus
4410 W. Easton Place
Tulsa, Oklahoma 74127
Hardy cacti and succulents; Catalog available

Earl May Seed & Nursery Company
Box 50, 208 N. Elm Street
Shenandoah, Iowa 51603
*Seeds, bulbs, perennials, trees,
shrubs, and supplies*

Meridian's Equipment
2055 Bee's Ferry Road
Charleston, South Carolina 29407
Tools

Messelaar Bulb Company
Box 269, County Road
Ipswich, Massachusetts 01938
Hardy and tender bulbs

Midwest Cactus
Box 163
New Melle, Missouri 63365
Hardy cacti; Catalog available

Milaeger's Gardens
4838 Douglas Avenue
Racine, Wisconsin 53402
Perennials and roses; Catalog available

J. E. Miller Nurseries
5060 West Lake Road
Canandaigua, New York 14424
Fruits, trees, and supplies

Mini-Roses
Box 4255, Station A
Dallas, Texas 75208
Miniature roses

Modern Farm
Box 1420
Cody, Wyoming 82414
Tools, supplies, and ornaments

Mo's Greenhouse
185 Swan River Road
Bigfork, Montana 5991
Perennials, ground covers, and alpines

Montrose Nursery
Box 957
Hillsborough, North Carolina 27278
Perennials; Catalog available

Moose Tubers
Box 1010
Dixmont, Maine 04932
Tender bulbs and potatoes; Catalog available

Moosebell Flower, Fruit,
& Tree Company
Route 1, Box 240
St. Francis, Maine 04774

Mt. Leo Nursery
Box 135, 603 Beersheba Street
McMinnville, Tennessee 37110
Evergreens, trees, shrubs and fruits

Musser Forests
Box 340, Route 119 North
Indiana, Pennsylvania 15710
Trees, shrubs, and ground covers

Nampara Gardens
2004 Golfcourse Road
Bayside, California 95524
Redwood furniture and ornaments

Native Gardens
Route 1, Box 494
Greenback, Tennessee 37742
*Nursery-propagated native plants
and seeds; Catalog available*

The Natural Gardening Company
27 Rutherford Avenue
San Anselmo, California 94960
Tools, supplies, and books; Catalog available

Natural Gardening Research Center
Box 149
Sunman, Indiana 47041
Organic supplies

Natural Gardens
113 Jasper Lane
Oak Ridge, Tennessee 37830
*Southeastern native plants
and information on butterfly
gardens; Catalog available*

Nature's Control
Box 35
Medford, Oregon 97501
Organic supplies

Nature's Garden Nursery
Route 1, Box 488
Beaverton, Oregon 97007
*Perennials, ferns, and rock
garden plants; Catalog available*

Necessary Trading Company
Box 305, 626 Main Street
New Castle, Virginia 24127
*Organic supplies, tools, and
books; Catalog available*

New York State Fruit Testing
Cooperative Association
Box 462
Geneva, New York 14456
Hardy fruits

Nichols Garden Nursery
1190 N. Pacific Highway
Albany, Oregon 97321
*Annual, everlastings, herb and
vegetable seeds, and supplies*

Walter Nicke Company
Box 433
Topsfield, Massachusetts 01983
*Tools and supplies;
Catalog available*

Nitron Industries
Box 400, 100 W. Rock Street
Fayetteville, Arizona 72702
Organic supplies, and tools

Nor'East Miniature Roses
58 Hammond Street
Rowley, Massachusetts 01969
Miniature roses

North American Wildflowers
38 Hillside Avenue
Atlantic Highlands, New Jersey 07716
Perennials and ground covers

North Country Organics
Route 5, Box 107
Newbury, Vermont 05051
Organic supplies and books

Nourse Farms
RFD, Box 485
South Deerfield, Massachusetts 01373
Tissue-cultured strawberries and fruits

Novelty Nurseries
Box 382
Novelty, Ohio 44072
Hardy ferns; Catalog available

Ohio Earth Food
13737 Duquette Avenue N. E.
Hartville, Ohio 44632
Organic supplies

Orchid Gardens
6700 Splithand Road
Grand Rapids, Minnesota 55744
Wildflowers and ferns; Catalog available

Oregon Bulb Farms
14071 N. E. Arndt Road
Aurora, Oregon 97002
Lilies; Catalog available

Oregon Miniature Roses
8285 S. W. 185th Avenue
Beaverton, Oregon 97007
Miniature roses

Organic Farm & Garden Supply
131 Organic Lane
West Columbia, South Carolina 29169
Organic supplies; Catalog available

Organic Pest Management
Box 55267
Seattle, Washington 98155
Organic supplies

Pacific Berry Works
Box 54, 963 Thomas Road
Bow, Washington 98232
''Day-neutral'' everbearing strawberries

Paradise Water Gardens
62 May Street
Whitman, Massachusetts 02382
Water lilies, aquatics, and supplies; Catalog available

Park Place
2251 Wisconsin Avenue N. W.
Washington, DC 20007
Furniture, lights, and ornaments; Catalog available

Park Seed Company
Box 46, Highway 254 North
Greenwood, South Carolina 29648
Seeds and plants; annuals, perennials, bulbs, everlastings, trees, shrubs, fruit, and herbs

Pinetree Garden Seeds
New Gloucester, Maine 04260
Vegetable, flower, and herb seeds, bulbs, books, and supplies

Pixie Treasures Miniature
Rose Nursery
4121 Prospect Avenue
Yorba Linda, California 92686
Miniature roses; Catalog available

Plant Collectibles
103 Kenview Avenue
Buffalo, New York 14217
Supplies and books; Catalog available

Plants of the Southwest
1812 2nd Street
Santa Fe, New Mexico 87501
Native plant seed for water-saving gardens and books; Catalog available

The Plow & Hearth
560 Main Street
Madison, Virginia 22727
Tools, furniture, and ornaments

Pony Creek Nursery
Tilleda, Wisconsin 54978
Shrubs, fruits, flower and vegetable seeds, books, and supplies

Pompeian Studios
90 Rockledge Road
Bronxville, New York 10708
Italian garden ornaments

Popovitch & Associates
346 Ashland Avenue
Pittsburgh, Pennsylvania 15228
Garden lights

Powell's Gardens
Route 3, Box 21
Princeton, North Carolina 27569
Perennials, dwarf conifers, trees, and shrubs; Catalog available

Prentiss Court Ground Covers
Box 8662
Greenville, South Carolina 29607
Ground covers

The Primrose Path
Route 2, Box 110
Scottsdale, Pennsylvania 15683
Perennials, rock garden, and woodland plants; Catalog available

Putney Nursery
Putney, Vermont 05346
Perennials, ferns, herbs, and wildflowers; Catalog available

Quality Cactus
Box 319
Alamo, Texas 78516
Cacti, succulents, and tropicals, including bananas; Catalog available

Quality Dutch Bulbs
Box 225, 50 Lake Drive
Hillsdale, New Jersey 07642
Hardy bulbs

Raindrip
Box 2173
Chatsworth, California 91313
Drip irrigation systems

Raintree Nursery
391 Butts Road
Morton, Washington 98356
Edible plants, books, and supplies

Rakestraw's Perennial Gardens
3094 S. Term Street
Burton, Michigan 48529
Perennials and dwarf conifers; Catalog available

Rasland Farm
NC 82 at US 13
Godwin, North Carolina 28344
Herbs and supplies; Catalog available

Rayner Bros.
Box 1617, Mt. Herman Road
Salisbury, Maryland 21801
Strawberries and other fruits

Reed Brothers
Turner Station
Sebastopol, California 95472
Redwood furniture; Catalog available

Replogle Globes
2801 S. 25th Avenue
Chicago, Illinois 60153
Sundials; Catalog available

Rider Nurseries
Route 2, Box 90A
Farmington, Iowa 52626
Strawberries and other fruits

Ringer Research
9959 Valley View Road
Eden Prairie, Minnesota 55344
Organic supplies and tools

Rocky Meadow Orchard & Nursery
Route 1, Box 104
New Salisbury, Indiana 47161
Fruit trees; Catalog available

The Rose Garden & Mini Rose Nursery
Box 560, Austin Street
Cross Hill, South Carolina 29332
Miniature roses

Rosehill Farm
Gregg Neck Road
Galena, Maryland 21635
Miniature roses

The Rosemary House
120 S. Market Street
Mechanicsburg, Pennsylvania 17055
Herbs and supplies; Catalog available

Roses by Fred Edmunds
6235 S. W. Kahle Road
Wilsonville, Oregon 97070
Roses

St. Lawrence Nurseries
Potsdam-Madrid Road
Potsdam, New York 13676
Hardy fruits

Sandy Mush Herb Nursery
Route 2, Surrett Cove Road
Leicester, North Carolina 28748
Herbs and seeds; Catalog available

Santa Barbara Water Gardens
Box 4353, 160 East Mountain Drive
Santa Barbara, California 93140
Water lilies and supplies; Catalog available

S. Scherer & Sons
104 Waterside Road
Northport, New York 11768
Water lilies, aquatics, and supplies

Sequoia Nursery
2519 East Noble Avenue
Visalia, California 93277
Miniature roses

Shady Oaks Nursery
700 19th Avenue N. E.
Waseca, Minnesota 56093
Plants for shade; Catalog available

Shepherd's Garden Seeds
7389 West Zayante Road
Felton, California 95018
European vegetable, flower, and herb seeds; Catalog available

R. H. Shumway Seedsman
Box 1
Graniteville, South Carolina 29829
Old-fashioned vegetable and flower seeds and fruits; Catalog available

Slocum Water Gardens
1101 Cypress Gardens Boulevard
Winter Haven, Florida 33880
Water lilies and aquatics; Catalog available

Smith & Hawken
25 Corte Madera
Mill Valley, California 94941
Tools, supplies, books, and furniture

Soergel Greenhouses
2573 Brandt School Road
Wexford, Pennsylvania 15090
Perennials

Southern Statuary and Stone
3401 Fifth Avenue S.
Birmingham, Alabama 35222
Furniture and ornaments; Catalog available

Stallings Exotic Nursery
910 Encinitas Boulevard
Encinitas, California 92024
Tropical plants and bulbs; Catalog available

Stocking Rose Nursery
785 N. Capitol Avenue
San Jose, California 95133
Roses

Stokes Seed Company
Box 548
Buffalo, New York 14240
Vegetable, flower, and herb seeds

Sunlight Gardens
Route 3, Box 286B
Loudon, Tennessee 37774
Wildflowers

Sunnybrook Farms Nursery
Box 6, 9448 Mayfield Road
Chesterland, Ohio 44026
Herbs and supplies; Catalog available

Sunnyvale Cactus Nursery
679 Pearl Street
Reading, Massachusetts 01867
Hardi cacti; Catalog available

Taylor's Herb Gardens
1535 Lone Oak Road
Vista, California 92084
Herb plants and seeds; Catalog available

Ter-El Nursery
Box 112
Orefield, Pennsylvania 18069
Ground covers ; Catalog available

Thomasville Nurseries
Box 7, 1842 Smith Avenue
Thomasville, Georgia 31799
Roses and plants for the South

Thompson & Morgan
Box 1308
Jackson, New Jersey 08527
Seeds of plants of all types

Tilley's Nursery/The Water Works
111 E. Fairmount Street
Coopersburg, Pennsylvania 18036
Water lilies, aquatics, and supplies; Catalog available

Tillinghast Seed Company
Box 738, 623 Morris Street
La Conner, Washington 98257
General nursery stock and seeds

Tiny Petals Nursery
489 Minot Avenue
Chula Vista, California 92010
Miniature roses

William Tricker, Inc.
7125 Tanglewood Drive
Independence, Ohio 44131
Water lilies and aquatics; Catalog available

Tripple Brook Farms
37 Middle Road
Southampton, Massachusetts 01073
Northeastern native and unusual plants

Turnipseed Nursery Farms
Box 792, 685 S. Glynn Street
Fayetteville, Georgia 30214
Ground covers

Otis Twilley Seed Company
Box 65
Trevose, Pennsylvania 19047
Vegetable and flower seeds

TyTy Plantation
Box 159
TyTy, Georgia 31795
Perennials and tender bulbs

Valley Creek Nursery
Box 364, 15177 S. Log Cabin Road
Three Oaks, Michigan 49128
Herbs, kiwis, and miniature roses

K. Van Bourgondien & Sons
Box A, 245 Farmingdale Road
Babylon, New York 11702
Tender and hardy bulbs, perennials, fruits, and shrubs

Van Ness Water Gardens
2460 North Euclid
Upland, California 91768
Water lilies, aquatics, and supplies; Catalog available

Vandenberg
3 Black Meadow Road
Chester, New York 10918
Hardy and tender bulbs; Catalog available

VanWell Nursery
Box 1339
Wenatchee, Washington 98801
Fruits

Vermont Bean Seed Company
Garden Lane
Fair Haven, Vermont 05743
Annual, perennial, herb, and vegetable seeds, and supplies

Andre Viette Farm & Nursery
Route 1, Box 16
Fishersville, Virginia 22939
Perennial plants, including ornamental grasses

Vintage Wood Works
Box 980
Fredericksburg, Texas 78624
Victorian gazebo and millwork; Catalog available

Walpole Woodworkers
767 East Street
Walpole, Massachusetts 02081
Cedar furniture and prefabricated buildings; Catalog available

Wyrttun Ward
18 Beach Street
Middleboro, Massachusetts 02346
Herbs, Northeastern wildflowers, and woodland and dye plants; Catalog available

Water Lily World
2331 Goodloe
Houston, Texas 77093
Water lilies and aquatics; Catalog available

Water Ways Nursery
Route 2, Box 247
Lovettsville, Virginia 22080
Water lilies and aquatics; Catalog available

Waterford Gardens
74 E. Allendale Road
Saddle River, New Jersey 07458
Water lilies and supplies; Catalog available

Waynesboro Nurseries
Box 987, Route 664
Waynesboro, Virginia 22980
Fruits, trees, shrubs, and ground covers

Wayside Gardens
Box 1
Hodges, South Carolina 29695
Trees, shrubs, vines, ground covers, perennials, roses, and supplies; Catalog available

We-Du Nurseries
Route 5, Box 724
Marion, North Carolina 28752
Rock garden and woodland plants; Catalog available

Well-Sweep Herb Farm
317 Mt. Bethel Road
Port Murray, New Jersey 07865
Herbs and supplies; Catalog available

White Flower Farm
Route 63
Litchfield, Connecticut 06759
Perennials, bulbs, trees, shrubs, and supplies; Catalog available

Wicklein's Aquatic Farm
& Nursery
1820 Cromwell Bridge Road
Baltimore, Maryland 21234
Water lilies, aquatics, and supplies; Catalog available

The Wildflower Source
Box 312
Fox Lake, Illinois 60020
Unusual woodland wildflowers, many propagated by tissue culture; Catalog available

Wildginger Woodlands
Box 1091
Webster, New York 14580
Rock garden and woodland plants; Catalog available

The Wildwood Flower
Route 3, Box 165
Pittsboro, North Carolina 27312
Nursery-propagated wildflowers; Catalog available

Willsboro Wood Products
Box 336
Willsboro, New York 12996
Cedar furniture

Winter Country Cacti
5405 Mohawk Road
Littleton, Colorado 80123
Hardy cacti and succulents; Catalog available

Winterthur Museum & Gardens
115 Brand Road
Salem, Virginia 24156
Plants and ornaments

Womack Nursery
Route 1, Box 80
DeLeon, Texas 76444
Fruits and some ornamentals, and pruning and grafting supplies; Catalog available

Wood Classics
Route 1, Box 455E
High Falls, New York 12440
Wooden furniture; Catalog available

Woodlanders
1128 Colleton Avenue
Aiken, South Carolina 29801
Southeastern native trees, shrubs, ground covers, and perennials, plus others; Catalog available

Wrenwood of Berkeley Springs
Route 4, Box 361
Berkeley Springs, West Virginia 25411
Herbs, perennials, and rock garden plants; Catalog available

Index

Limonium sinuatum, 47, 75
Lindera benzoin, 30, 70
Lisianthus. *See Eustoma grandiflorum*
Lizard's-tail. *See Saururus cernuus*
Lobularia maritima, 19, 21, 54
Loebner magnolia. *See Magnolia x loebneri*
Lonicera periclymenum, 73
Lonicera tatarica, 55, 70
Lonicera x brownii, 70, 73
Lonicera x heckrottii, 73
Lovage. *See Levisticum officinale*
Love-in-a-mist. *See Nigella damascena*
Lunaria annua, 47
Lungwort. *See Pulmonaria arenaria*
Lycopersicon lycoperscum, 27, 53, 75

Madagascar periwinkle. *See Catharanthus roseus*
Magnolia x loebneri, 55
Maidenhair fern. *See Adiantum pedatum*
Malabar spinach. *See Basella alba*
Malus sylvestris, 34
Malva alcea, 25
Maple. *See Acer ginnala; Acer platanoides*
Marginal shield. *See Dryopteris marginalis*
Marigold. *See Calendula officinalis; Tagetes erecta; Tagetes patula; Tagetes tenuifolia*
Marjoram. *See Origanum majorana*
Marrubium incanum, 75
Martha Washington's plume. *See Filipendula rubra*
Matteuccia struthiopteris, 47, 59, 78
Mazzard cherry. *See Prunus avium*
Mealycup sage. *See Salvia farinacea*
Melissa officalis, 75
Mentha spicata, 54, 75
Mentha suaveolens, 75
Mentor barberry. *See Berberis x mentorensis*
Menyanthes trifoliata, 50
Mertensia virginica, 30
Merton foxglove. *See Digitalis x mertonensis*
Meserve holly. *See Ilex x meserveae*
Meyer lilac. *See Syringa meyeri*
Milfoil. *See Myriophyllum acquaticum*
Miniature rose. *See Rosa* sp.

Miscanthus sinensis, 25, 28, 46, 65
Mock orange. *See Philadelphus coronarius*
Molinia caerulea, 28
Moluccella laevis, 47
Monarda didyma, 15, 16, 25, 77
Money plant. *See Lunaria annua*
Monkshood. *See Aconitum carmichaelii*
Moonflower. *See Ipomoea alba*
Moor grass. *See Molinia caerulea*
Morning-glory. *See Ipomeoea purpurea*
Mother-of-thyme. *See Thymus praecox*
Mountain alyssum. *See Alyssum montanum*
Mountain ash. *See Sorbus alnifolia*
Mountain pink. *See Pius mugo*
Mugwort. *See Artemisia schmidtiana*
Musa acuminata, 66
Myrica pensylvanica, 48
Myriophyllum aquaticum, 50

Nannyberry. *See Viburnum lentago*
Narrow eastern cedar. *See Juniperus virginiana*
Narrow western cedar. *See Juniperus scopulorum*
Nasturtium. *See Tropaeolum majus*
Nepeta mussinuii, 15, 75
Nephrolepsis exaltata, 53
Nicotiana alata, 19, 21, 25, 36, 53
Nigella damascena, 47, 75
Nippon spiraea. *See Spiraea nipponica*
Norway maple. *See Acer platanoides*
Nymphaea sp., 50

Oat grass. *See Helicotrichon sempervirens*
Ocimum basilicum, 19, 21, 27, 54, 75
Okra. *See Abelmoschus esculentus*
Opuntia erinacea, 43
Opuntia fragilis, 43
Opuntia humifusa, 43
Opuntia polyacantha, 43
Opuntia whipplei, 43
Oregano. *See Origanum vulgare*
Oriental bittersweet. *See Celastrus orbiculatus*
Oriental lily. *See Lilium* sp.
Oriental poppy. *See Papaver orientale*

Origanum dictamnus, 75
Origanum majorana, 27, 75
Origanum vulgare, 75
Ornamental pepper. *See Capsicum annuum*
Osmunda cinnamomea, 30, 45, 66, 78
Osmunda regalis, 78
Ostrich fern. *See Matteuccia struthiopteris*
Our-lady's bedstraw. *See Galium verum*

Pachysandra terminalis, 81
Paeonia lactiflora, 25
Painted daisies. *See Chrysanthemum coccineum*
Pak-choi. *See Brassica rapa*
Papaver nudicaule, 36
Papaver orientale, 25
Parsley. *See Petroselinum crispum*
Parthenocissus tricuspidata, 66, 73
Peach-bell. *See Campanula persicifolia*
Pear. *See Pyrus communis*
Pediocactus simpsonii, 43
Peegee hydrangea. *See Hydrangea paniculata*
Pelargonium graveolens, 54, 75
Pelargonium peltatum, 19
Pelargonium x hortorum, 19, 21, 25, 25, 54
Pennisetum alopecuroides, 15, 28
Pennyroyal. *See Mentha pulegium*
Peony. *See Paeonia lactiflora*
Pepper. *See Capsicum annuum*
Perilla fratescens, 75
Periwinkle. *See Catharanthus roseus; Vinca minor*
Persian centaurea. *See Centaurea hypoleuca*
Petroselinum crispum, 27, 54, 75
Petunia x hybrida, 19, 21, 25, 53, 54, 69
Phacelia campanularia, 19, 21
Phalaris arundinacea, 28, 65
Phaseolus coccineus, 73
Phaseolus lunatus, 73
Phaseolus vulgaris, 27, 73
Philadelphus coronarius, 55, 70
Phlox divaricata, 30
Phlox subulata, 32
Physalis alkekengi, 46
Physocarpus opulifolius, 48

Physotegia virginiana, 16, 25
Picea abies, 32, 54, 59, 62, 81
Picea glauca, 16, 39
Pickerel rush. *See Pontederia cordata*
Pigmy tuna. *See opuntia fragilis*
Pincushion flower. *See Scabiosa altropurpurea; Scabiosa caucasica*
Pineapple mint. *See Mentha suaveolens*
Pineapple-scented sage. *See Salvia elegans; Salvia rutilans*
Pink-flowering locust. *See Robinia x ambigua*
Pink lady's-slipper. *See Cypripedium acaule*
Pinus bungeana, 45, 59
Pinus mugo, 81
Pisum sativum, 27, 54, 73
Plain's prickly pear. *See Opuntia polyacantha*
Plantain lily. *See Hosta sieboldiana; Hosta* sp.; *Hosta ventricosa*
Platycodon grandiflorus, 15, 16, 25, 32, 36
Pole bean. *See Phaseolus vulgaris*
Polygonatum biflorum, 30
Polygonatum odoratum, 25, 77
Polygonum aubertii, 73
Polystichum acrostichoides, 30, 77, 78
Pontederia cordata, 50
Poppy. *See Papaver nudicaule; Papaver orientale*
Potentilla fruticosa, 12, 48, 55
Poterium sanguisorba, 75
Pot marigold. *See Calendula officinalis*
Prickly pear. *See Opuntia humifusa*
Primula veris, 75
Proboscidea louisianica, 47
Prunus avium, 65
Prunus cerasus, 34, 54
Pulmonaria. *See Symphytum grandiflorum*
Pulmonaria arenaria, 77
Purple cauliflower. *See Brassica oleracea*
Purple coneflower. *See Echinacea purpurea*
Purple-leaf smokebush. *See Cotinus coggygria*
Purple trillium. *See Trillium erectum*
Pussy-toes. *See Antennaria dioica*
Pussy willow. *See Salix discolor*
Pyrus calleryana, 60, 69
Pyrus communis, 36